SCIENCE Fusion

fusion [FYOO • zhuhn] a combination of two or more things that releases energy

This Write-In Student Edition belongs to

_____

Teacher/Room

_____

 HOUGHTON MIFFLIN HARCOURT

HOUGHTON MIFFLIN HARCOURT

Front Cover: *lion* ©Cesar Lucas Abreu/Stone/Getty Images; *grass* ©Nicholas Eveleigh/Stockbyte/Getty Images; *tulips* ©John McAnulty/Corbis; *soccer* ©Jon Feingersh Photography, Inc./Blend Images/Getty Images; *volcano* ©Westend 61 GmbH/Alamy; *microscope* ©Thom Lang/Corbis.

Back Cover: *guitar* ©Brand Z/Alamy; *giraffe* ©Nicholas Eveleigh/Stockbyte/Getty Images; *observatory* ©Robert Llewellyn/Workbook Stock/Getty Images; *wind turbine* ©Comstock/Getty Images.

Printed in the U.S.A.

ISBN 978-0-547-57772-2

12 13 14 15 0928 20 19 18 17 16 15

4500548223   BCDEFG

Consulting Authors

Michael A. DiSpezio
Global Educator
North Falmouth, Massachusetts

Marjorie Frank
Science Writer and Content-Area Reading Specialist
Brooklyn, New York

Michael Heithaus
Director, School of Environment and Society
Associate Professor, Department of Biological Sciences
Florida International University
North Miami, Florida

Donna Ogle
Professor of Reading and Language
National-Louis University
Chicago, Illinois

Program Advisors

Paul D. Asimow
Professor of Geology and Geochemistry
California Institute of Technology
Pasadena, California

Bobby Jeanpierre
Associate Professor of Science Education
University of Central Florida
Orlando, Florida

Gerald H. Krockover
Professor of Earth and Atmospheric Science Education
Purdue University
West Lafayette, Indiana

Rose Pringle
Associate Professor
School of Teaching and Learning
College of Education
University of Florida
Gainesville, Florida

Carolyn Staudt
Curriculum Designer for Technology
KidSolve, Inc.
The Concord Consortium
Concord, Massachusetts

Larry Stookey
Science Department
Antigo High School
Antigo, Wisconsin

Carol J. Valenta
Associate Director of the Museum and Senior Vice President
Saint Louis Science Center
St. Louis, Missouri

Barry A. Van Deman
President and CEO
Museum of Life and Science
Durham, North Carolina

Power up with Science Fusion!

Your program fuses...

e-Learning & Virtual Labs

Labs & Activities

Write-In Student Edition

... to generate new science energy for today's science learner—**you**.

Write-In Student Edition

STEM activities throughout the program!

Be an active reader and make this book your own!

Write your ideas, answer questions, make notes, and record activity results right on these pages.

Learn science concepts and skills by interacting with every page.

It's Your M...

Objects can move in many way... They can move in a straight line,... back and forth, or round and rou...

Trace the dashed lines below to ...ow ...e ways objects can move.

zigzag

...aigh...

bac...

Labs & Activities

Science is all about doing.

Exciting investigations for every lesson.

How Are Plants of the Same Kind Different?

Observe plants to compare and contrast them. How are plants of the same kind different?

Materials
bunch of carrots

1. Observe the carrots to see how they are different. Caution! Do not eat the carrots.

2. Draw and write your observations.

3. Compare your drawings. How can carrots be different from one another?

Ask questions and test your ideas.

Draw conclusions and share what you learn.

e-Learning & Virtual Labs

Digital lessons and virtual labs provide e-learning options for every lesson of *Science Fusion*.

On your own or with a group, explore science concepts in a digital world.

360° of Inquiry

Contents

LIFE SCIENCE

Unit 3—Animals

PHYSICAL SCIENCE

Unit 9—All About Matter......................323

How Scientists Work

Children's Museum,
Indianapolis, Indiana

Big Idea

Scientists use inquiry skills and tools to help them find out information.

I Wonder Why

Scientists study dinosaurs. Why?
Turn the page to find out.

Here's Why Scientists study dinosaurs to learn about animals that lived long ago.

In this unit, you will explore this Big Idea, the Essential Questions, and the Investigations on the Inquiry Flipchart.

Levels of Inquiry Key ■ DIRECTED ■ GUIDED ■ INDEPENDENT

Track Your Progress

Big Idea Scientists use inquiry skills and tools to help them find out information.

Essential Questions

Now I Get the Big Idea!

Science Notebook
Before you begin each lesson, be sure to write your thoughts about the Essential Question.

Essential Question

What Are Senses and Other Tools?

🧠 Engage Your Brain!

Find the answer to the question in the lesson.

What sense is this child trying <u>not</u> to use?

the sense of

_____

Active Reading

Lesson Vocabulary

1 Preview the lesson.

2 Write the 2 vocabulary terms here.

_____   _____

Your Senses

How do you learn about things? You use your five senses. Your **senses** are the way you learn about the world. The senses are sight, hearing, smell, taste, and touch. You use different body parts for different senses.

Active Reading

The main idea is the most important idea about something. Draw two lines under the main idea.

You hear with your ears.

You smell with your nose.

You taste with your mouth.

You touch with your hands and skin.

You see with your eyes.

► Circle the name of the body parts you use for each sense.

Learning with Your Senses

How can your senses help you learn? Look at the pictures. What would your senses tell you about each thing?

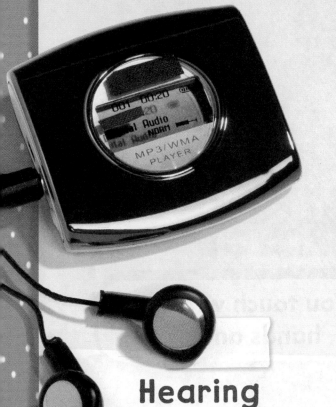

Hearing
You listen to learn how things sound.

Touching
You touch to learn about texture—how things feel.

▶ **Underline how you learn how things feel.**

Seeing

You use sight to observe color, shape, and size.

Smelling

You use smell to learn how things smell.

Tasting

You taste to learn if foods are sweet, sour, or salty.

▶ You use sight to observe three things. Circle the words.

Tools to Explore

You can use science tools to learn more. People use **science tools** to find out about things.

A hand lens is a science tool. It helps you see small things. You could not see these things as well with just your eyes.

Active Reading

Find the sentence that tells about **science tools**. Draw a line under the sentence.

These children are using a hand lens to closely observe a flower.

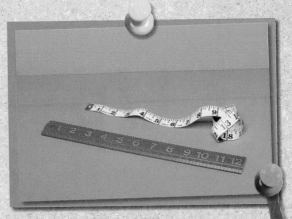

Ruler and Tape Measure

A ruler measures how long things are. A tape measure measures around things.

Measuring Cup

A measuring cup measures liquids.

Tools for Measuring

▶ Circle the names of tools you use to measure.

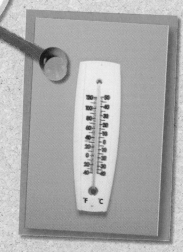

Balance

A balance compares how heavy things are.

Thermometer

A thermometer measures temperature. It tells how hot and cold things are.

Measuring Up

Why should we use science tools to measure? What would happen if we used different things to measure the same object? We might get different measurements.

> **This girl is using her shoes to measure the rug.**

Do the Math!

Measure Length

Measure how long a bookcase is. Use a small shoe, a large shoe, and a tape measure or a ruler. The tape measure or ruler measures in feet.

How long is the bookcase when you measure

1. with a small shoe?

   about _____ small shoes long

2. with a big shoe?

   about _____ big shoes long

3. with a ruler or tape measure?

   about _____ feet long

Why should you use a ruler or a tape measure to measure the bookcase?

_____

_____

_____

_____

Sum It Up!

① Choose It!

Which tool is <u>not</u> used to measure? Mark an X on it.

② Circle It!

Which tool helps you observe small things? Circle it.

③ Match It!

Look at each thing. Which sense helps you learn about it? Draw lines to match them.

You touch to feel how furry something is.

You see to read.

You smell food baking.

Name _____

Word Play

You use different body parts for different senses. Label each body part with its sense.

| hearing | sight | smell | taste | touch |

Apply Concepts

Draw a line to the picture whose name completes the sentence.

1. Measure a ball with a _____.

2. Measure water with a _____.

3. Observe an ant with a _____.

4. Compare how heavy with a _____.

5. Measure length with a _____.

Take It Home! **Family Members:** Ask your child to tell how we use science tools and our senses to learn about the world. Play a game to name the senses or tools you use in different situations.

Name _____

Essential Question

How Can We Use Our Senses?

Set a Purpose
Tell what you want to find out.

_____

Think About the Procedure
❶ What will you observe?

_____

_____

❷ How will you find out the sound of breaking celery?

_____

_____

Record Your Data

In this chart, record what you observe.

Sense	Observation
Sight	
Touch	
Smell	
Hear	
Taste	

Draw Conclusions

What did you find out about celery? How do you know?

_____

_____

Ask More Questions

What other questions could you ask about celery and your senses?

_____

_____

Essential Question

What Are Inquiry Skills?

Engage Your Brain!

Find the answer to the question in the lesson.

What can you infer this boy is doing?

The boy is

_____

Active Reading

Lesson Vocabulary

1 Preview the lesson.

2 Write the vocabulary term here.

_____

Skills to Help You Learn

Observe and Compare

How can you be like a scientist? You can use inquiry skills. **Inquiry skills** help you find out information. They help you learn about your world.

Active Reading

You can compare things. You find ways they are alike. A child on this page is comparing two things. Draw a triangle around the two things.

Falling Leaves Forest

observe

compare

Predict and Measure

measure

predict

Rocky Cliff

▶ Circle the inquiry skill that helps you find the size of an object.

Classify and Communicate

Bird
Paradise

classify

▶ **Complete the graph. How many brown birds are there?**

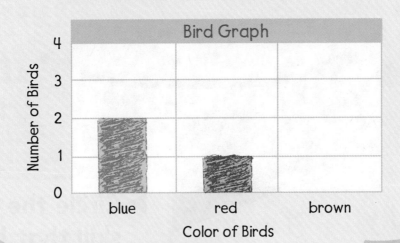

Bird Graph

Number of Birds

4
3
2
1
0

blue   red   brown

Color of Birds

communicate

Hypothesize and Plan an Investigation

hypothesize   plan an investigation

Rolling Logs Hill

▶ Which child made a hypothesis? Draw a line under the hypothesis.

Infer and Draw Conclusions

I think the
light container
is empty.

Picnic
Palace

infer

Empty containers
are lighter than
full containers.

draw conclusions

▶ Underline the
conclusion the
child drew.

22

Make a Model and Sequence

Butterfly Garden

▶ Things may happen in order.
Write 1 beside what happens first.
Write 2 beside what happens second.
Write 3 beside what happens third.
Write 4 beside what happens last.

make a model

sequence

Sum It Up!

① Circle It!

You want to learn about something. Circle what you do to find out.

predict

classify

plan an investigation

② Choose It!

What inquiry skill does this show?

communicate

make a model

sequence

③ Draw It!

Observe an object. Draw it. Tell about it.

This is a _____. It is _____.

Name _____

Word Play

Circle the letters to spell the words. Then complete the sentence.

compare	classify	infer	measure
observe	predict	sequence	

```
s  e  q  u  e  n  c  e  a
v  c  l  a  s  s  i  f  y
u  l  r  i  n  f  e  r  t
r  m  e  a  s  u  r  e  p
o  b  s  e  r  v  e  g  e
e  w  p  r  e  d  i  c  t
c  o  m  p  a  r  e  t  z
```

All the words in the puzzle are _____ .

Apply Concepts

Circle the word that matches the meaning.

1 tell what you learn	communicate	observe
2 sort things into groups	sequence	classify
3 tell how things are alike and different	make a model	compare
4 put things in order	sequence	hypothesize
5 find out how much or how long	measure	infer
6 use your senses	make a model	observe
7 make a good guess about what will happen	predict	sequence
8 decide what steps to follow	draw conclusions	plan an investigation

© Houghton Mifflin Harcourt Publishing Company

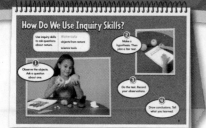

Name _____

Essential Question

How Do We Use Inquiry Skills?

Set a Purpose

Tell what you want to find out.

_____

_____

_____

Think About the Procedure

❶ What fair test did you plan? Write your plan here.

_____

_____

❷ What science tools will you use for your test?

_____

Record Your Data

Draw or write. Record what you observe.

Draw Conclusions

What conclusions can you draw?

_____

_____

Ask More Questions

What other questions could you ask?

_____

_____

How Do Scientists Work?

Engage Your Brain!

Find the answer to the question in the lesson.

How do you paint a rainbow using only three colors of paint?

You can mix

_____

Active Reading

Lesson Vocabulary

1 Preview the lesson.

2 Write the vocabulary term here.

_____

Think Like a Scientist

Scientists plan an investigation when they want to learn more. An **investigation** is a test scientists do. There are different plans for investigations. Here is one plan.

Observe

First, observe something. Ask a question about it.

Active Reading

Clue words can help you find the order of things. **First** is a clue word. Draw a box around this clue word.

What would happen if we mixed yellow paint and blue paint?

Hypothesize and Make a Plan

Next, make a hypothesis. State something you can test. Plan a fair test to see whether you are correct.

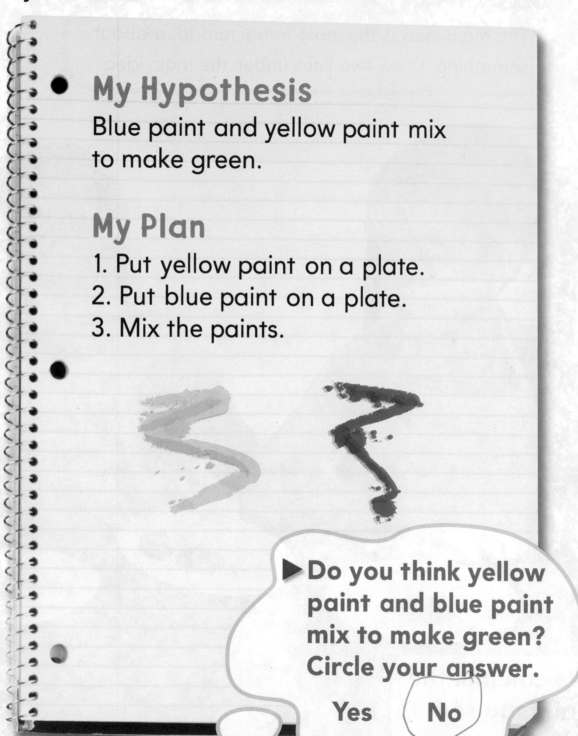

My Hypothesis

Blue paint and yellow paint mix to make green.

My Plan

1. Put yellow paint on a plate.
2. Put blue paint on a plate.
3. Mix the paints.

▶ **Do you think yellow paint and blue paint mix to make green? Circle your answer.**

Yes   No

Do the Test

Do the test. Follow the steps of your plan. Observe what happens.

Active Reading

The main idea is the most important idea about something. Draw two lines under the main idea.

We can mix the paints to see what happens.

Draw Conclusions

Draw conclusions from your test. What did you learn? Compare your results with your classmates' results. What would happen if you did the test again? How do you know?

If we do the test again, yellow paint and blue paint will still make green.

▶ Circle the color that yellow and blue make when you mix them.

33

Record What You Observe

Scientists record what they learn from an investigation. You can keep a record in a science notebook. You can draw pictures. You can write.

Active Reading

A detail is a fact about a main idea. Draw one line under a detail. Draw an arrow to the main idea it tells about.

▶ **What colors make green?**

Sum It Up!

① Write It!

You have a ⬛ and a ⬛.
You will drop them.
You think the block will fall faster.
How can you test your idea?

_____

② Circle It!

You do the steps in an investigation.
Now you draw what happens.
Which step are you doing?
Circle it.

Observe.   Plan a fair test.

Record what you observe.

Name _____

Word Play

Unscramble the word to complete each sentence. Use these words if you need help.

observe   hypothesize   investigation   record

ntiovetigansi

① To learn more about something, you do an _____.

eyhtpoheszi

② When you make a statement you can test, you _____.

dreorc

③ After you do a test, you should _____ your results.

beosver

④ When you look at something closely, you _____ it.

Can air move a penny and a feather?
Tell how you could investigate.
Write a number from 1 to 5 to show the order.

_____ Write a plan.

_____ Ask a question–
Can air move a penny and a feather?

_____ Record what you observe.

_____ Share your results.

_____ Follow your plan.

Take It Home!

Family Members: Ask your child to tell you about the steps of an investigation. Then plan an investigation you and your child can try at home.

Learn About...
Mary Anderson

In 1902, Mary Anderson observed something. In bad weather, drivers had trouble seeing. They had to drive with the window open. Or they had to get out to clean off the windshield. Anderson got an idea. She invented the windshield wiper.

Drivers could use it from inside their vehicle. They could see the road and stay warm and dry.

Fun Fact

By the 1920s all cars had windshield wipers.

This Leads to That

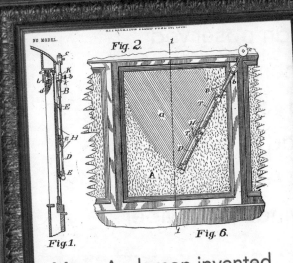

Mary Anderson invented the first windshield wiper. This shows an early drawing.

Robert Kearns invented a windshield wiper that went on and off as needed.

▶ **How does Mary Anderson's invention help people today?**

_____

_____

_____

Unit 1 Review

Vocabulary Review

Use the terms in the box to complete the sentences.

> inquiry skills
> investigation
> senses

1. You learn about the world by using your _____.

2. To find out information, you use _____.

3. To learn more, scientists plan an _____.

Science Concepts

Fill in the letter of the choice that best answers the question.

4. What can you learn from listening to music?
   Ⓐ how it feels
   Ⓑ how it looks
   Ⓒ how it sounds

5. You want to find out which toy car goes a greater distance. What question do you ask?
   Ⓐ Why do cars roll?
   Ⓑ Which car is older?
   Ⓒ Which car will roll farther?

6. Which sense is the boy using to observe the flower?

Ⓐ hearing
Ⓑ smell
Ⓒ taste

7. You do a fair test and draw the results. What are you doing?
Ⓐ classifying
Ⓑ communicating
Ⓒ measuring

8. You want to measure the length of a leaf. Which science tool will you use?

Ⓐ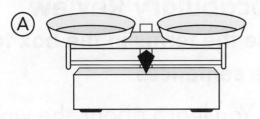

Ⓑ

Ⓒ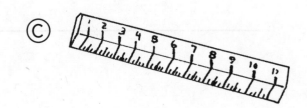

9. You tell what happens first, next, and last in an activity. Which inquiry skill is this?

Ⓐ hypothesize

Ⓑ infer

Ⓒ sequence

10. Which step in an investigation is shown?

Ⓐ doing a test

Ⓑ drawing a conclusion

Ⓒ recording results

11. What do you do when you classify?

Ⓐ group things by how they are alike

Ⓑ tell what you think will happen

Ⓒ use observations to tell why something happens

12. You and a classmate compare your results. The results are not the same. What should you do?

Ⓐ repeat the test

Ⓑ tell your teacher

Ⓒ throw away the results

Inquiry and the Big Idea
Write the answers to these questions.

13. Look at this picture.

a. What sense is the girl using?

_____

b. What can she learn by petting the dog?

_____

14. You want to investigate how fast two toy cars roll. Your hypothesis is that a metal car rolls faster than a wooden car. What steps would you follow to test your hypothesis?

_____

_____

_____

© Houghton Mifflin Harcourt Publishing Company

Technology All Around Us

© Houghton Mifflin Harcourt Publishing Company (bkgd) ©Jeff Greenberg/Alamy (border) ©NDIsc/Age Fotostock

Big Idea

Engineers use a process to design and build something new. They use many different kinds of materials.

children's playground

I Wonder How

An engineer planned a design for this playground. How?

Turn the page to find out.

Here's How An engineer drew ideas on a plan. The plan had many fun things for kids.

In this unit, you will explore this Big Idea, the Essential Questions, and the Investigations on the Inquiry Flipchart.

Levels of Inquiry Key ■ DIRECTED ■ GUIDED ■ INDEPENDENT

Track Your Progress

Big Idea Engineers use a process to design and build something new. They use many different kinds of materials.

Essential Questions

Now I Get the Big Idea!

Science Notebook

Before you begin each lesson, be sure to write your thoughts about the Essential Question.

Essential Question

How Do Engineers Work?

Engage Your Brain!

Find the answer to the question in the lesson.

How do you scratch an itch you can not reach?

You can

_____

_____.

Active Reading

Lesson Vocabulary

1 Preview the lesson.

2 Write the 2 vocabulary terms here.

_____ _____

Problem Solvers

An **engineer** uses math and science to solve everyday problems. Engineers work on many kinds of problems. Some engineers design robots. Others plan roads. Some design cars.

▶ Circle the names of three kinds of engineers.

robotics engineer

Engineers use a design process to solve problems. A **design process** is a plan with steps that help engineers find good solutions.

The Design Process

1. Find a Problem
2. Plan and Build
3. Test and Improve
4. Redesign
5. Communicate

mechanical engineer

civil engineer

The Design Process

Find a Problem

Jack has an itch he can not reach. How can he scratch it? The steps of this design process show Jack what to do.

Jack names his problem. He needs to find a way to scratch his back. He brainstorms ways to solve his problem.

Jack tries to scratch his back.

▶ **What problem does Jack want to solve?**

_____

_____

Jack gets out his science notebook.
He wants to record what he does to solve
his problem.

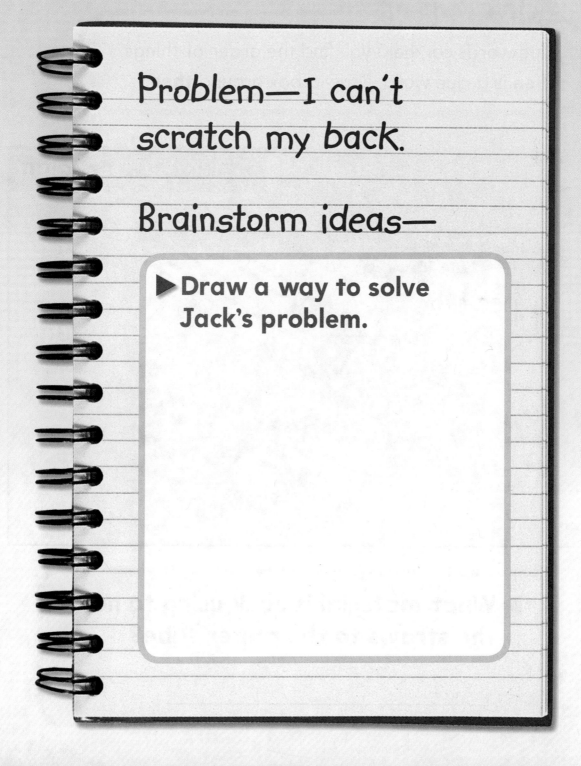

Problem—I can't scratch my *back*.

Brainstorm ideas—

▶ **Draw a way to solve Jack's problem.**

Then Jack chooses a solution to try.
He makes a plan. Jack draws and labels his
plan. He chooses the best materials to use.

Active Reading

Clue words can help you find the order of things.
Then is a clue word. Draw a box around **then**.

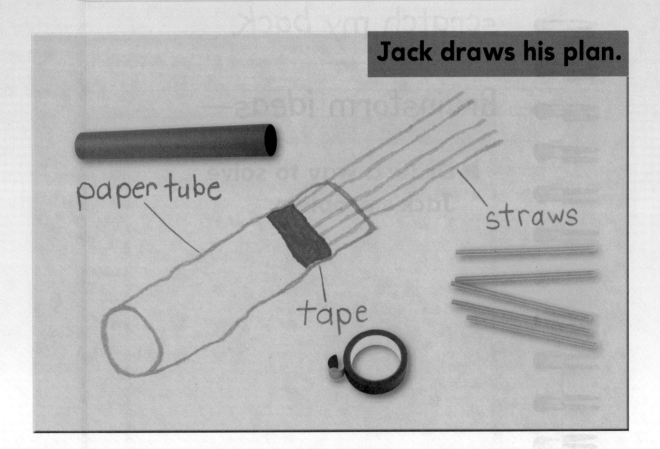

Jack draws his plan.

paper tube

straws

tape

▶**What material is Jack using to hold
the straws to the paper tube?**

_____

Jack builds his back scratcher.
He uses the materials he chose and the
plan he made.

Jack makes his
back scratcher.

Test and Improve

Jack tests the back scratcher with a friend. They try the back scratcher to see whether it works. Does the back scratcher solve the problem?

▶ **Write a way to improve the design of the back scratcher.**

_____

_____

Jack and a friend test the back scratcher.

4 Redesign

Jack thinks of a way to redesign his back scratcher. He adds notes about how to make it better.

How to make it better—Replace the straws with sticks to scratch harder.

paper tube

straws

tape

5 Communicate

Jack writes and draws to show what happened. He can share what he learned with others.

▶ **Which material is Jack using to make his design better? Circle the word.**

Sum It Up!

① Circle It!

Circle the step of the design process shown in the picture.

How to make it better—
Replace the straws with
sticks to scratch harder.

paper tube

straws

tape

Find a Problem

Plan and Build

Redesign

② Solve It!

Answer the riddle.

I solve problems using science and math. The design process leads me along the right path.

Who am I?

_____

56

Name _____

Word Play

Write a label for each picture.

choose materials   build   engineer   test

_____   _____

_____   _____

Write numbers to put the steps of the design process in order. The first one is done for you.

The Design Process

_____ Test and Improve

____1____ Find a Problem

_____ Communicate

_____ Redesign

_____ Plan and Build

Family Members: Help your child identify a problem at home, such as a messy "junk drawer." Have your child guide you through the design process to find a solution.

Name _____

Essential Question

How Can We Solve a Problem?

Set a Purpose

Tell what you will do.

_____

_____

Think About the Procedure

1 What steps will you follow to build your stand?

_____

_____

2 How will you know that your stand works?

_____

Record Your Data

Draw and label a picture that shows what happened.

[ ]

Draw Conclusions

How did your solution work? How could you redesign the stand to make it better?

_____

_____

Ask More Questions

What other questions could you ask about designing a solution to a problem?

_____

Essential Question

What Materials Make Up Objects?

Engage Your Brain!

Find the answer to the question in the lesson.

What could you make with this wood?

_____

Active Reading

Lesson Vocabulary

1 Preview the lesson.

2 Write the 3 vocabulary terms here.

_____   _____

_____

Play Your Part

Objects may be made of different parts. The parts go together to make the whole.

Look at this bicycle. It has wheels, a frame, and other parts. These parts go together to make a bicycle.

Active Reading

A detail is a fact about a main idea. Draw a line under a detail. Draw an arrow to the main idea it tells about.

_____

wheel
_____

_____

► Write labels for the parts of the bicycle.

bicycle

A Material World

Look at this house. One part is brick. Another part is metal. Other parts are wood. The windows are glass.

Brick, metal, wood, and glass are materials. **Materials** are what objects are made of.

Active Reading

Find the sentence that tells the meaning of **materials**. Draw a line under the sentence.

brick

wood

glass

metal

▶ Write labels to name four materials in this house.

65

Made to Order

Materials are natural or human-made. **Natural** materials are found in nature. For example, cotton is from a plant. Wood is from trees. Metal comes from rocks.

People make **human-made** materials such as plastics and nylon. Scientists first made them in a lab. Scientists changed petroleum into these new materials not found in nature.

trees

cotton

Crude Oil

petroleum

cotton shirt

wooden boat with nylon sail

Some objects are made of natural materials. Others are made of human-made materials. Some objects are made of both natural and human-made materials.

▶ **Mark an X on the object made from both natural and human-made materials.**

plastic toys

Everyday Materials

Do you have a pair of jeans? Cotton jeans are made in factories. Here is how.

Active Reading

Things may happen in order. Draw a line under the step that happens first.

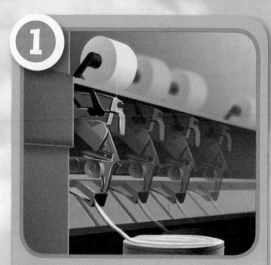

1 Looms weave cotton into cloth.

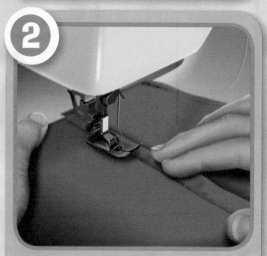

2 Workers use machines to cut and sew the cloth.

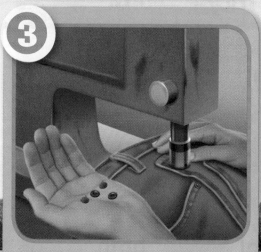

3 Workers use machines to put on metal rivets.

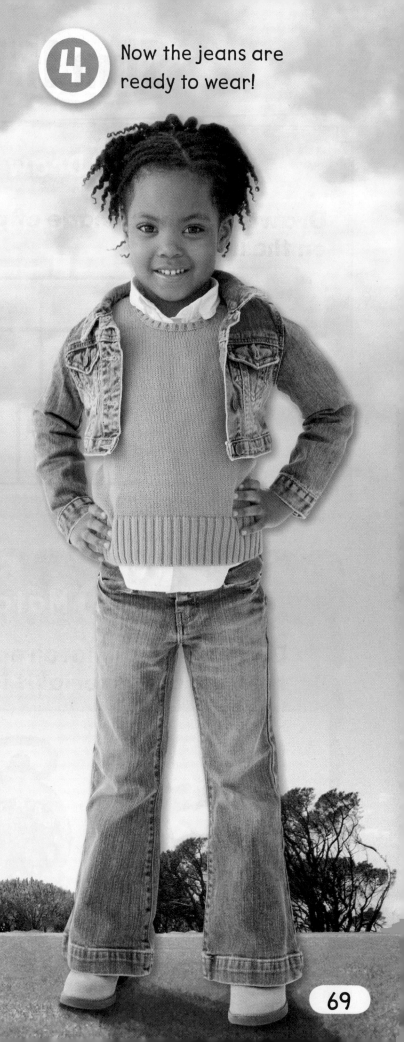

4 Now the jeans are ready to wear!

① Draw It!

Draw something made of glass on the house.

② Match It!

Draw a line to match each toy with the kind of material it is made from.

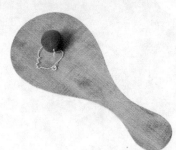

human-made   natural   both

Brain Check

Name _____

Word Play

Color the letters to spell the vocabulary words. Write the words to complete the sentences.

human-made	materials	natural

n	a	t	u	r	a	l	t	w	k
c	t	o	w	r	e	g	y	p	s
h	u	m	a	n	m	a	d	e	y
g	m	a	t	e	r	i	a	l	s
k	n	y	u	o	s	d	x	p	m

1 Objects are made of _____.

2 Materials made in a lab are _____.

3 Materials found in nature are _____.

Apply Concepts

Complete the chart. Name and classify the materials each object is made from.

Materials Chart

Object	Material	Natural, human-made, or both
1	_____ _____	_____
2	_____ _____	_____
3	_____ _____	_____

Family Members: Play a game with your child to identify the parts and materials of objects around the home. Classify the materials as natural, human-made, or both.

Take It Home!

Name _____

Essential Question

How Can Materials Be Sorted?

Set a Purpose

Tell what you want to do.

_____

Think About the Procedure

❶ What will you observe about the objects?

_____

_____

❷ How will you sort the objects?

_____

_____

Record Your Data

Draw or write to show how you sorted the objects.

Natural	Human-made	Both

Draw Conclusions

How could you tell what objects were made of?

_____

_____

Ask More Questions

What other questions could you ask about objects and materials?

_____

_____

_____

Get to Know
Dr. Eugene Tsui

Dr. Eugene Tsui is an architect. This is a kind of engineer. An architect designs homes and other buildings.

Dr. Tsui studies forms in nature, such as sea shells. He bases his designs on what he learns. Dr. Tsui says that nature is our great teacher.

Fun Fact

Dr. Tsui also designs his own clothes.

Dr. Tsui's Designs

▶ **Draw a line from each building to the natural form it is based on.**

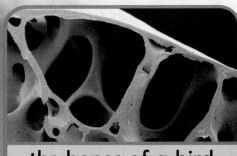

the bones of a bird

fish scales

dragonfly wings

▶ **Think about a form from nature. Use it to design your own building.**

Vocabulary Review

Use the terms in the box to complete the sentences.

| engineer |
| materials |
| natural |

1. Someone who uses math and science to solve everyday problems is an _____.

2. An object is made of its _____.

3. Something that is made from things found in nature is _____.

Science Concepts

Fill in the letter of the choice that best answers the question.

4. A cotton shirt has a metal zipper. What kinds of materials make up the shirt?

Ⓐ natural

Ⓑ human-made

Ⓒ both natural and human-made

5. Loveleen wants to build a feeder that many birds can use. How can she follow the design process?

Ⓐ buy a new bird feeder

Ⓑ plan and build a solution

Ⓒ tell a friend about the feeder

6. Cara is playing with two toys.

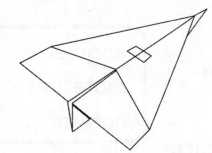

Which toy is made from a human-made material?

Ⓐ the paper airplane

Ⓑ the plastic bucket

Ⓒ both are made from human-made materials

7. Which is **true** of all engineers?

Ⓐ All engineers build roads.

Ⓑ All engineers design cars.

Ⓒ All engineers solve problems.

8. Which object is made from natural materials?

Ⓐ a nylon shirt

Ⓑ a plastic bottle

Ⓒ a wood table

9. What is the **first** step of the design process?

Ⓐ Find a Problem

Ⓑ Plan and Build

Ⓒ Test and Improve

10. A river is between two towns. People want to drive from one town to the other. Two engineers talk about the problem.

How do they plan to solve it?

Ⓐ build a tunnel under the river

Ⓑ build a bridge over the river

Ⓒ give boats to the people in the towns

11. You draw a picture of something you designed.

What step of the design process is this?

Ⓐ Communicate

Ⓑ Redesign

Ⓒ Test and Improve

12. Which object is made of both natural materials and human-made materials?

Ⓐ a metal bucket with a wooden handle

Ⓑ a wood door with a metal handle

Ⓒ a cotton bag with a plastic handle

Inquiry and the Big Idea
Write the answers to these questions.

13. Geeta sorted objects into these two groups.

Group 1	Group 2
wood pencil	plastic toy
sheet of paper	nylon jacket

a. How did she sort the objects?

_____

_____

b. Name one thing that could be added to each group.

_____

14. Cold air is coming in under Michael's door. He wants to use the design process to find a solution.

a. What should Michael do first?

_____

b. Michael builds a tool. How can he test it?

_____

c. What should he do if the tool does not work?

_____

UNIT 3
Animals

Big Idea

All animals have to meet needs in order to live and grow.

spoonbill carrying a twig

I Wonder Why

This bird is carrying a twig. Why?
Turn the page to find out.

Here's Why A spoonbill builds its nest from sticks and twigs. The nest is a safe place for the spoonbill's chicks.

In this unit, you will explore this Big Idea, the Essential Questions, and the Investigations on the Inquiry Flipchart.

Levels of Inquiry Key ■ DIRECTED ■ GUIDED ■ INDEPENDENT

Track Your Progress

Big Idea All animals have to meet needs in order to live and grow.

Essential Questions

Now I Get the Big Idea!

Science Notebook

Before you begin each lesson, be sure to write your thoughts about the Essential Question.

Essential Question

What Are Living and Nonliving Things?

Engage Your Brain!

Find the answer to the question in the lesson.

What do all living things need?

_____

Active Reading

Lesson Vocabulary

1 Preview the lesson.

2 Write the 4 vocabulary terms here.

_____ _____

_____ _____

Living It Up!

Living things are people, animals, and plants. They need food, water, air, and space to live. They grow and change. Living things **reproduce**. They make new living things like themselves.

flowers

► **Label the living things you see in the picture.**

groundhog

What's Nonliving?

Nonliving things do not need food, air, and water. They do not grow and change. What are some nonliving things? A rock is a nonliving thing. Air and water are nonliving things, too.

Active Reading

Find the sentences that tell the meaning of **nonliving things**. Draw a line under them.

▶ **List nonliving things you see.**

_____

_____

_____

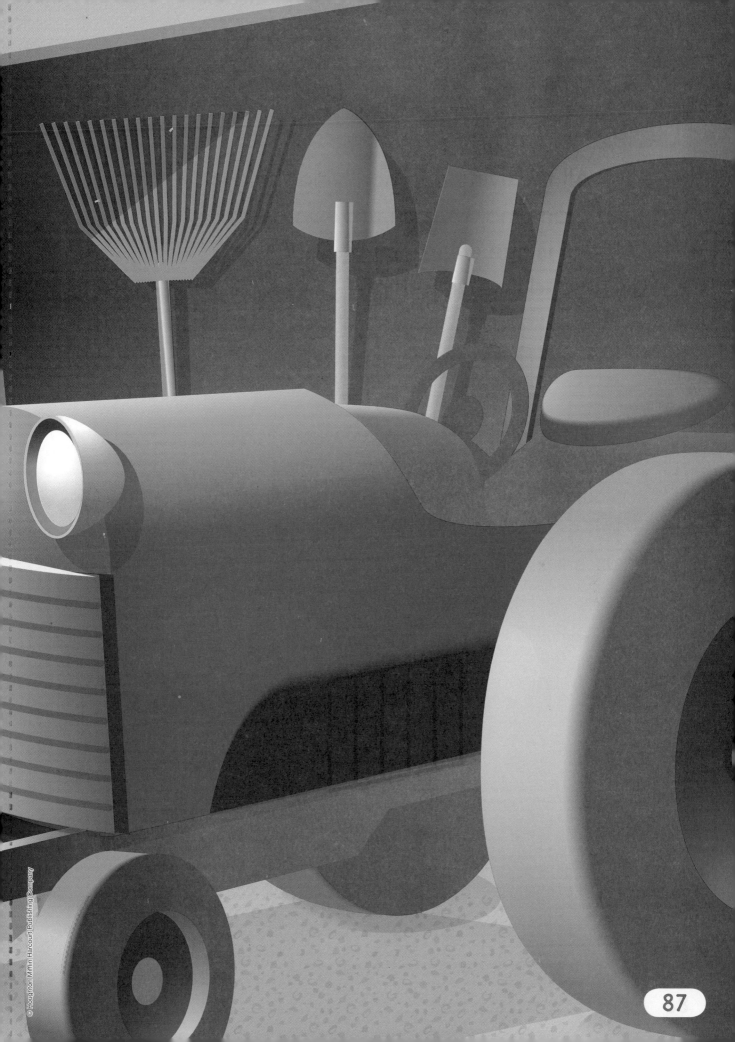

All Together

All the living and nonliving things in a place make up an **environment**. A farm is one environment. It has living and nonliving things.

Active Reading

The main idea is the most important idea about something. Draw two lines under the main idea.

▶List living and nonliving things you see in a farm environment.

Living	Nonliving

Sum It Up!

① Choose It!

Circle each living thing.
Draw an X on each nonliving thing.

② Draw It!

Draw a living thing and a nonliving thing you might find in a park.

Name _____

Word Play

Color the living things. Circle the nonliving things.

Complete the chart. Show how living and nonliving things are different.

Living Things	Nonliving Things
① grow and change	do not grow and change
② _____	do not reproduce
③ need air	do not need _____
④ need _____	do not need water
⑤ need food	do not need _____

Look around your environment. Name one living thing and one nonliving thing.

Living Thing	Nonliving Thing
⑥ _____	⑦ _____

Family Members: Take a survey of your home with your child. List the living things and the nonliving things you see.

Essential Question

What Do Animals Need?

🧠 Engage Your Brain!

Find the answer to the question in the lesson.

Why is a clownfish shelter unusual?

A clownfish lives

_____.

Active Reading

Lesson Vocabulary

❶ Preview the lesson.

❷ Write the 2 vocabulary terms here.

_____ _____

Food and Water

Animals need food and water to grow and stay healthy. Some animals eat plants. Some eat other animals. Still others eat both plants and animals.

The main idea is the most important idea about something. Draw two lines under the main idea.

A deer drinks water.

Air

Animals need oxygen, a gas in air. Land animals use their lungs to breathe in oxygen. Some water animals, like whales, have lungs. They breathe air. Fish do not have lungs. They use **gills** to get oxygen.

A black bear uses its lungs to breathe.

gills

A fish uses gills to take in oxygen from the water.

▶ Which animal uses its gills to get oxygen?

_____

Shelter

Most animals need shelter. A **shelter** is a place where an animal can be safe. An animal may use a plant as a shelter. It may dig a hole in the ground. It may even use another animal as a shelter. One animal that does this is a clownfish.

Kinds of Animal Shelters

A prairie dog lives in a burrow.

A beaver lives in a lodge.

Some birds lay eggs
in a nest.

A skunk lives
in a den.

▶ Draw an animal
in its shelter.

Space

Animals need space to grow. They need space to move around and find food. Animals need space for shelter. They need space to take care of their young.

Active Reading

A detail is a fact about a main idea. Draw one line under a detail. Draw an arrow to the main idea it tells about.

A cheetah needs space to run and catch its food.

Your Needs

You are a living thing. You must meet your needs to grow and stay healthy. What do you and other people need? You need air to breathe. You need food and water. You need space and shelter.

▶ **How are the needs of people like the needs of animals?**

_____

_____

Caring for Pets

Pets are animals. Think about some pets you know. Where do they get their food and water? Who gives them shelter? They need people to help them meet their needs.

Taking care of a pet is a big job. A pet needs space to exercise and play. You need to keep the pet and its shelter clean. You must clean up after a pet, too.

100

People need to take care of pets and keep them clean.

People need to give pets food.

This dog gets 1 cup of dog food in the morning and 1 cup of dog food at night.

How many cups of dog food does it get for 1 day?

1 cup in morning
+ 1 cup at night
_____

_____ cups in one day

How many cups of dog food does it get for 5 days?

_____

Sum It Up!

① Choose It!

Mark an X on the need that does <u>not</u> belong.

Animal Needs

water   sunlight

air   food

② Circle It!

How are people and animals alike?

They both need soil.

They both live in dens.

They both need sunlight.

They both need air and water.

③ Draw It!

Draw the animal you might find in each shelter.

nest

burrow

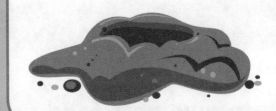

Name _____

Word Play

Pets need things to help them live and grow.
Fill in the words to tell what a hamster needs.

air   food   shelter   space to grow   water

a_____

w_____

s_____

s_____   f_____

Apply Concepts

Think about how you meet your needs each day. Then fill in the chart below.

You Need	How You Meet Your Needs
❶ air	_____
❷ _____	I drink from the water fountain at soccer practice.
❸ food	_____
❹ _____	I go inside my house when it rains.
❺ space to grow	_____

Take It Home!

Family Members: Discuss with your child what animals and people need to grow and stay healthy. Ask your child to tell you how his or her needs are met.

Tool Time

How We Use Tools

Tools are objects that people use to make a job easier. People can use tools to meet needs.

One need is shelter. A shelter may be a house. People use many tools to build a house.

drill

hammer

The Best Tool for the Job

Draw a line to match each tool to how it is used.

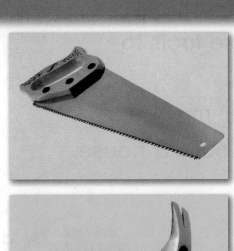

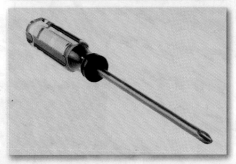

S.T.E.M.
continued

Build On It!

You can design your own tool. Complete **Design It: A New Tool** on the Inquiry Flipchart.

Essential Question

How Are Animals Different?

Engage Your Brain!

Find the answer to the question in the lesson.

This animal is not an insect. What is it?

_____

Active Reading

Lesson Vocabulary

1 Preview the lesson.

2 Write the 6 vocabulary terms here.

_____   _____

_____   _____

_____   _____

sloth

All Kinds of Animals

Animals have different shapes and sizes. They have body parts that help them move in different ways. Some animals walk and run. Others fly or swim.

Animals have different body coverings. Some have fur or hair. Others have scales or feathers.

Active Reading

Clue words can help you find ways things are different. **Different** is a clue word. Draw a box around this word.

© Houghton Mifflin Harcourt Publishing Company (bkgd) ©Joel Santore/Getty Images

Ways to Group Animals

feathers

scarlet macaw

fur

spider monkey

swim
river dolphin

climb

red-eyed tree frog

big

capybara

small

leaf-cutter ants

▶ Circle the words that help group animals by the way they move.

golden lion tamarin

giant anteater

Mammals

A **mammal** has fur or hair. Most mammals have live young. A young mammal drinks milk from its mother's body. People are mammals.

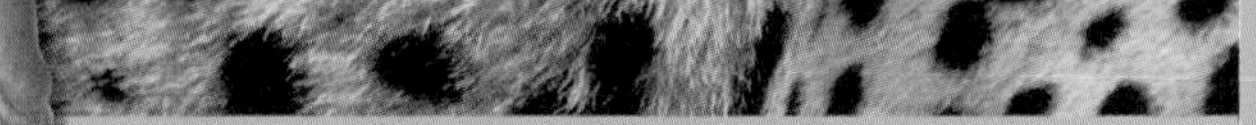

▶ Label the body covering you see.

_____

jaguar

quetzal

toucan

Birds

A **bird** has feathers. Birds also have a beak and wings. Most birds use wings to fly. Birds lay eggs. They find food to feed their young.

▶ Label the body covering you see.

parrot

_____

Reptiles

A **reptile** has dry skin. It is covered in scales. Most reptiles lay eggs.

Most reptiles have four legs. But snakes are reptiles with no legs. Turtles are reptiles. They may have legs or flippers. A turtle also has a shell on its back.

green iguanas

caiman

▶ Label the body covering you see.

_____

Amphibians

Most **amphibians** have smooth, wet skin. Toads are amphibians with rough, bumpy skin.

Amphibians lay their eggs in water. Young amphibians live in the water. Most grown amphibians live on land.

poison dart frog

cane toad

▶ Label the body covering you see.

_____

Fish

Fish have body parts that help them live in water. Most **fish** have scales. The scales help keep their bodies safe. Fish have fins to swim. They have gills to take in oxygen.

Active Reading

The main idea is the most important idea about something. Draw two lines under the main idea.

red piranha

silver dollar fish

▶ **Label the body covering you see.**

_____

grasshopper

butterfly

Insects

An **insect** has three body parts and six legs. A hard shell keeps its body safe.

Some animals look like insects, but they are not. A spider has eight legs. It is not an insect.

▶ **Label the body covering you see.**

_____

rhinoceros beetle

Sum It Up!

1 Mark It!

Draw an X on the animal that is **not** a mammal.

Circle the animal that is an amphibian.

2 Draw It!

Two animal groups have scales. Draw an animal from each group. Label it.

Name _____

Word Play

Unscramble the letters to name six animal groups.

reptile mammal fish amphibian insect bird

lammam   __ (__) __ __ __ __

esctni   __ (__) __ __ __ __

drib   __ (__) __ __

phibiaman   __ (__) __ __ __ __ __ __ (__) __

plitree   __ __ __ __ __ (__) __

isfh   __ __ (__) __

Write the circled letters in order to complete the sentence.

There are many different kinds

of _____ .

117

Apply Concepts

Draw or write an animal from each group.

Animal Groups

Animal Group	Animal from That Group
❶ mammal	
❷ bird	
❸ reptile	
❹ amphibian	
❺ fish	
❻ insect	

Take It Home!

Family Members: Discuss animal groups with your child. Look through magazines and help your child group the animals you see.

118

Name _____

Essential Question
How Can We Group Animals?

Set a Purpose
Tell what you want to find out.

_____

_____

Think About the Procedure
1 How do you know which animals belong in the same group?

_____

_____

2 How will you record the groups you make?

_____

Record Your Data

Color a box to show each way the animal moves.

How Does It Move?

	Walk	Swim	Fly
duck			
butterfly			
mouse			
fish			
bat			
penguin			
parrot			
alligator			
cow			

Draw Conclusions

How could you tell how an animal moves?

Ask More Questions

What other questions can you ask about classifying animals?

Picture Cards

Cut out each picture on the dashed lines.

duck

butterfly

mouse

fish

bat

penguin

parrot

alligator

cow

121

Picture Cards

Cut out each picture on the dashed lines.

Lesson 4

mouse

butterfly

duck

penguin

bat

fish

cow

alligator

parrot

Ask a Zoo Keeper

What does a zoo keeper do?

I feed the animals. I give them water. I make sure that the animals are healthy. I also keep their environments clean.

How do you know when an animal is sick?

Animals can not tell me when they don't feel well. So I observe them carefully. Sometimes an animal eats or moves very little. That could be a sign that the animal is sick.

What else does a zoo keeper do?

I talk to people about the zoo animals. I have fun talking to children. They like animals so much!

Now It's Your Turn!

▶ **What question would you ask a zoo keeper?**

_____

_____

Now You Be a Zoo Keeper!

▶ A tiger cub was born at your zoo. Make a plan to take care of the cub.

My Zoo Keeper Plan

 1 I will _____

_____.

 **2** I will _____

_____.

 3 I will _____

_____.

Unit 3 Review

Vocabulary Review

Use the terms in the box to complete the sentences.

> amphibian
> gills
> reproduce

1. A fish takes in oxygen with its

   _____.

2. An animal with smooth, wet skin is

   an _____.

3. When animals make new living things
   like themselves, they

   _____.

Science Concepts

**Fill in the letter of the choice that best
answers the question.**

4. How are all animals
   the same?

   Ⓐ All animals need food
      and water.

   Ⓑ All animals live in the
      same place.

   Ⓒ All animals move in
      the same way.

5. Which animals need air
   to live?

   Ⓐ No animals need air
      to live.

   Ⓑ All animals need air
      to live.

   Ⓒ Only land animals
      need air to live.

6. An animal does **not** get food, air, and water. What will happen?

   Ⓐ The animal will die.

   Ⓑ The animal will become a plant.

   Ⓒ The animal will be healthy and survive.

7. What kind of animal does this picture show?

   Ⓐ birds

   Ⓑ insects

   Ⓒ mammals

8. Which of these animals gives birth to live young?

   Ⓐ

   Ⓑ

   Ⓒ

9. What do all the living and nonliving things in a place make up?

    Ⓐ an environment

    Ⓑ a basic need

    Ⓒ a shelter

10. Which is **true** about an animal you keep as a pet?

    Ⓐ It does not have basic needs.

    Ⓑ It needs people to help it meet its needs.

    Ⓒ It does not need shelter or food.

11. How are birds and reptiles alike?

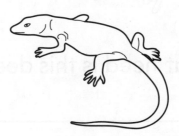

    Ⓐ They both lay eggs.

    Ⓑ They both have scales.

    Ⓒ They both have feathers.

12. How are living things **different** from nonliving things?

    Ⓐ Living things may be large or small.

    Ⓑ Living things need food and water.

    Ⓒ Living things may be in many places.

Inquiry and the Big Idea
Write the answers to these questions.

13. Look at this deer.

a. What need is this deer meeting?

_____

b. Name two other needs the deer has.

_____

c. What happens to the deer if its basic needs are not met?

_____

14. Name one living and one nonliving thing you might find in your backyard. How do you know which is living and which is nonliving?

_____

_____

_____

_____

© Houghton Mifflin Harcourt Publishing Company

Plants

Big Idea

Plants have parts to help them meet their basic needs. There are many kinds of plants.

grapes growing on a vine

I Wonder Why
Grapes need water, light, and air. Why?
Turn the page to find out.

129

Here's Why All plants need water, light, and air to make food.

In this unit, you will explore this Big Idea, the Essential Questions, and the Investigations on the Inquiry Flipchart.

Levels of Inquiry Key ■ DIRECTED ■ GUIDED ■ INDEPENDENT

Big Idea Plants have parts to help them meet their basic needs. There are many kinds of plants.

Essential Questions

Now I Get the Big Idea!

Science Notebook

Before you begin each lesson, be sure to write your thoughts about the Essential Question.

Essential Question

What Do Plants Need?

🧠 Engage Your Brain!

Find the answer to the question in the lesson.

How does this plant grow without soil?

Its roots take in

_____

_____ .

Active Reading

Lesson Vocabulary

1 Preview the lesson.

2 Write the 3 vocabulary terms here.

_____   _____

_____

Plant Needs

Sunlight, Air, and Water

A plant needs certain things to live and grow. A plant needs **sunlight**, or light from the sun. It also needs air and water. A plant uses these things to make its food.

Active Reading

The main idea is the most important idea about something. Draw two lines under the main idea.

Air is all around us, even though we can not see it.

Plants grow toward the sun to get the light they need.

Plants get most of the water they need from the soil.

▶ **Circle three words that name things a plant needs.**

From the Soil

Most plants need soil to grow. **Soil** is made up of small pieces of rock and once-living things. A plant's roots take in water from the soil. The roots take in nutrients, too. **Nutrients** are things in soil that help plants grow.

Some plants do not grow in soil. They live and grow on other plants. Their roots take in rain and water from the air.

Active Reading

A detail is a fact about a main idea. Draw one line under a detail. Draw an arrow to the main idea it tells about.

Space to Grow

As a plant grows, its stem gets taller. Its roots get bigger. It grows more leaves, too. A plant must have enough space to grow.

▶ **What does this farmer do to make sure that his crop grows?**

_____

_____

_____

People Helping Plants

How do people help plants? They water plants. They pull weeds so plants have space to grow. People put plants by windows so the plants can get sunlight.

Active Reading

Clue words can help you find an effect. **So** is a clue word. Draw a box around **so**.

People also help plants by planting new ones. They plant seeds so new flowers can grow. They plant young trees so people can enjoy them.

▶ **How do you help plants?**

_____

_____

Sum It Up!

① Circle It!

Circle two things that a plant needs.

② Write It!

This plant has gotten too big for its pot.

What need is not being met?

_____

 **Brain Check**

Name _____

Word Play

Write each word next to the part of the picture it tells about.

| water | sunlight | soil | air |

_____

_____

_____

Answer the question.

What things in soil help plants grow?

_____

Apply Concepts

Complete the web to tell what plants need to grow and be healthy.

Plant Needs

Take It Home!

Family Members: Ask your child to tell you about the things a plant needs to grow and be healthy. Talk about how your family or someone your family knows helps plants.

Name _____

Essential Question
Why Do Plants Grow?

Set a Purpose
Tell what you want to find out.

_____

_____

Think About the Procedure
❶ What will you observe?

_____

_____

❷ How will you treat the plants differently?

_____

_____

Record Your Data

In this chart, record what you observe.

My Observations of Two Plants		
	Plant A	**Plant B**
How the stems look		
How the leaves look		
Other observations		

Draw Conclusions

Can a plant grow when it does not get what it needs?

_____

_____

Ask More Questions

What other questions could you ask about plant needs?

_____

_____

Essential Question

What Are Some Parts of Plants?

 **Engage Your Brain!**

Find the answer to the question in the lesson.

What holds this tree in place?

its _____

Active Reading

Lesson Vocabulary

1 Preview the lesson.

2 Write the 6 vocabulary terms here.

_____   _____

_____   _____

_____   _____

A Plant's Makeup

A plant has parts that help it grow and change.

Taking Root

A plant has roots that grow into the soil. The **roots** hold the plant in place. They take in water from the soil. They take in other things from the soil that the plant needs.

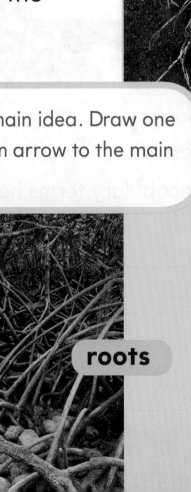

roots

Stems Stand Tall

The **stem** holds up the plant. It takes water from the roots to the other parts of the plant.

A flower has a thin, soft stem. A tree has a thick, woody stem.

stems

▶ **Draw a triangle around the roots of the bean plant. Draw a circle around the stem.**

Leaves at Work

A **leaf** is a plant part that makes food for the plant. It uses light, air, and water.

Active Reading

Find the sentence that tells the meaning of **leaf**. Draw a line under the sentence.

Leaves can be different shapes and sizes.

banana leaf

pine needles

clover

ash

red maple

Flowers, Seeds, and Fruit

Many plants have flowers. A **flower** is a plant part that makes seeds. A new plant may grow from a **seed**. The new plant will look like the plant that made the seed.

Many flowers grow into fruits. A **fruit** holds seeds.

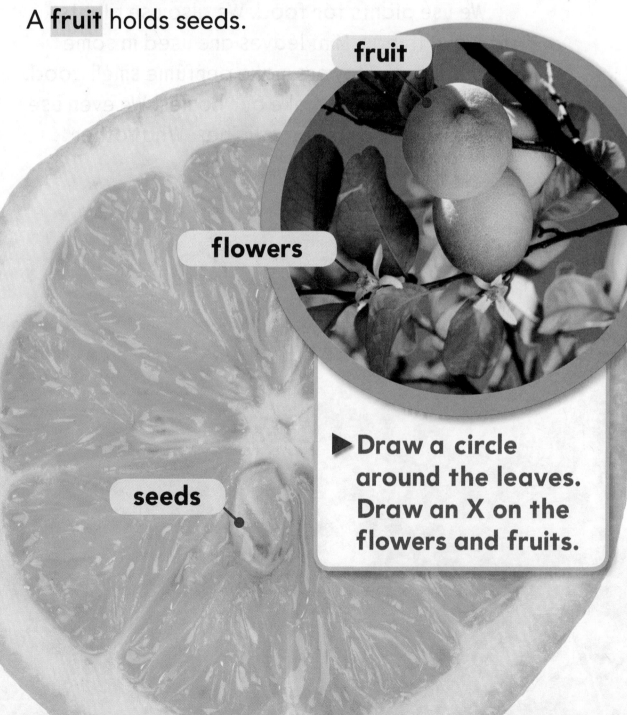

fruit

flowers

seeds

▶ **Draw a circle around the leaves. Draw an X on the flowers and fruits.**

Plant Power

We use plants for food. We also use plants to make things. Mint leaves are used in some toothpastes. Flowers make perfume smell good. Woody stems help make our homes. We even use plants to make some medicines. What other plant uses can you name?

Do the Math!
Solve a Problem

Look at the tomatoes. Use them to help you solve this problem.

A farmer has 24 tomatoes.
He picks 11 tomatoes.
How many are left?

_____ - _____ = _____

① Choose It!

Circle the plant part that takes in water.

② Solve It!

Solve each riddle.

I can be thick or thin.
I can be short or tall.
I help a plant get
water and hold it up so
it won't fall.

What am I?

_____

I can be different colors,
shapes, and sizes.
I may fall to the ground.
I take in light and air to
make food for a plant
since it can't move around.

What am I?

_____

Name _____

Word Play

Label the parts of the plant.

| flower | leaf | roots | stem |

_____

_____

_____

_____

Apply Concepts

Tell which plant parts the plant needs.

Problem	Solution
❶ I need a plant part to hold seeds. What part do I need?	_____
❷ I need a plant part to take in water. What part do I need?	_____
❸ I need a plant part to make fruit. What part do I need?	_____
❹ I need a plant part to make food. What part do I need?	_____
❺ I need a plant part to hold me up. What part do I need?	_____
❻ I need a plant part to make a plant just like me. What part do I need?	_____

Take It Home!

Family Members: Encourage your child to tell you about the parts of the plant. Help your child name plants you eat and use.

Get to Know ...
Dr. Norma Alcantar

Dr. Norma Alcantar studies materials. She makes them more useful. Dr. Alcantar wanted to find a way to make water clean.

She learned that some people in Mexico used prickly pear cactus plants to clean water. The plants have a gooey material. Dr. Alcantar studied it. She used the goo to make water clean.

Fun Fact

She learned about using this kind of cactus from her grandmother.

Clean It!

▶ **Answer the questions about Dr. Alcantar's work.**

1
What does
Dr. Alcantar study?

_____

_____

2
Where did Dr. Alcantar
get the idea for using
the prickly pear cactus
in her studies?

_____

_____

3
Why is Dr. Alcantar's
work important?

_____

_____

4
What does Dr. Alcantar
use from the cactus to
make clean water?

_____

How Are Plants Different?

Engage Your Brain!

Find the answer to the question in the lesson.

How is this plant like some animals?

_____

_____ .

Active Reading

Lesson Vocabulary

1 Preview the lesson.

2 Write the 2 vocabulary terms here.

_____   _____

Is It a Plant?

Plants are living things, like animals. Plants are also different from animals.

Plants can not move like animals. They stay in one place. Green plants use light, water, and air to make their own food. Animals eat plants or other animals.

Active Reading

When you compare things, you find out ways they are alike. Draw triangles around two things that are being compared.

Plants and Animals

▶ Complete the chart to tell how plants and animals are different.

	Plants	Animals
make their own food		
eat plants or animals		
move around on their own		
grow and change		

A Venus flytrap is a strange plant. It moves its leaves to catch insects and spiders. Then it eats what it catches.

Plenty of Plants

How can you tell plants apart? They have different leaves. They have different shapes. They can be big or small. Some plants have soft, thin stems. Some have thick, woody stems.

Trees
- tall
- woody trunk
- many branches
- different leaves
- long life

oak tree

Shrubs

- shorter than trees
- smaller, woody stems
- smaller branches
- different leaves
- long life

boxwood shrub

Grasses

- small plants
- soft stems
- long, thin leaves
- shorter life

ornamental grasses

▶ Circle the names of the plants with woody stems. Draw a line under the name of the plant with soft stems.

Plants with ✿ Flowers

Some plants have flowers. **Flowers** make a plant's seeds. Flowers can grow on small plants. They can also grow on shrubs and trees. Where have you seen flowers?

hibiscus plant

▶ **What do flowers do?**

_____

Plants with Cones

Some plants have cones. **Cones** hold a plant's seeds. Cones grow on some trees. Where have you seen cones?

Active Reading

A detail is a fact about a main idea. Draw one line under a detail. Draw an arrow to the main idea it tells about.

pinecone

pine tree

Sum It Up!

① Circle It!

Circle the plant that has cones.

② Choose It!

Circle each group of words that tells about an animal.

eats plants or animals

makes its own food

grows and changes

moves around on its own

③ Solve It!

Solve the riddle.

Some living things fly.
Some walk, run, or swim.
I do not move on my own.
I stay in one place.

What am I? _____

Brain Check

Name _____

Word Play

Color the letters to spell the vocabulary words.
Write the words to complete the sentences.

c	t	o	t	r	e	e
f	l	o	w	e	r	o
t	a	g	l	d	e	i
e	j	c	o	n	e	b
i	r	s	w	g	h	l
k	e	m	e	o	a	d
r	s	h	r	u	b	Y

flower   shrub
cone   tree

❶ A tall plant with a woody stem
is a _____ .

❷ A tree without a flower may have
a _____ .

❸ A _____ makes seeds.

❹ A plant that is smaller than a tree
is a _____ .

Apply Concepts

Complete the diagram to tell how plants and animals are alike and different.

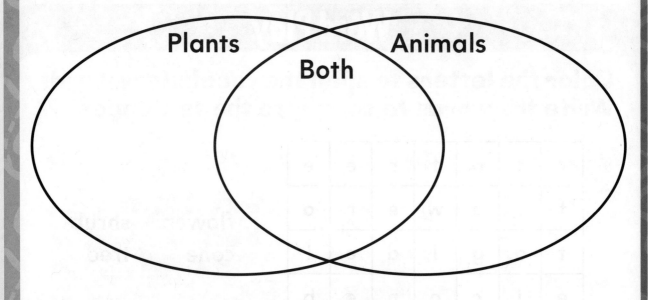

Plants   Both   Animals

① How can plant stems be different?

_____

_____

② Write 1, 2, and 3 to put the plants in size order.

Start with the smallest plant.

____ tree   ____ grass   ____ shrub

Take It Home!

Family Members: Take a neighborhood walk with your child. Ask your child to tell you how the plants you see are alike and different.

Name _____

Essential Question

How Can We Compare Leaves?

Set a Purpose

Tell what you want to find out.

_____

_____

Think About the Procedure

1 Why do you measure each leaf?

_____

2 How will you compare the leaves by size?

_____

_____

Record Your Data

Draw each leaf. Record its length. Then circle the shortest leaf. Draw an X on the longest leaf.

Leaf Chart

Leaf 1	Leaf 2	Leaf 3
about _____ paper clips long	about _____ paper clips long	about _____ paper clips long

Draw Conclusions

How could you tell for sure which leaf was the longest?

_____

_____

Ask More Questions

What other questions could you ask about comparing leaves?

_____

Warm It Up

Compare Greenhouses

Greenhouses are made of glass or plastic. Glass and plastic let in light. They also keep in heat. Light and heat help plants grow. Different plants can be grown at the same time.

indoor greenhouse

outdoor greenhouse

- needs only a small space
- for small plants only
- stays warm in winter

- needs a large space
- for small or large plants
- needs heating in winter

Which Greenhouse?

Read the sentences below.
Then answer the questions.

You want to grow a large plant.
You have a lot of outdoor space.
The weather is not very cold.
Which greenhouse would you
choose? Why?

_____

_____

_____

_____

Build On It!

 Design your own indoor greenhouse. Complete
Design It: Greenhouse on the Inquiry Flipchart.

Unit 4 Review

Vocabulary Review

Use the terms in the box to complete the sentences.

> leaf
> nutrients
> roots

1. Two things from soil that help a plant grow are water and _____.

2. A plant is held in place by its _____.

3. The plant part that makes food is the _____.

Science Concepts

Fill in the letter of the choice that best answers the question.

4. How are an apple and a pinecone **alike**?
   - Ⓐ They both are fruits.
   - Ⓑ They both hold seeds.
   - Ⓒ They both grow on the same kind of tree.

5. How could you find out if plants need light to live?
   - Ⓐ Grow two plants. Give both plants water.
   - Ⓑ Grow two plants. Give only one plant light.
   - Ⓒ Grow two plants. Give only one plant water.

6. Pavil sorted leaves. This picture shows one group.

Which choice **best** describes how she sorted?

Ⓐ by size
Ⓑ by shape
Ⓒ by number of points

7. Which of these plant parts is a kind of stem?
Ⓐ apple
Ⓑ tree trunk
Ⓒ pine needle

8. A plant needs more space to grow. Which would give the plant more space?
Ⓐ giving it more water
Ⓑ putting more plants around it
Ⓒ pulling up weeds around it

9. Which plant part does Number 3 show?

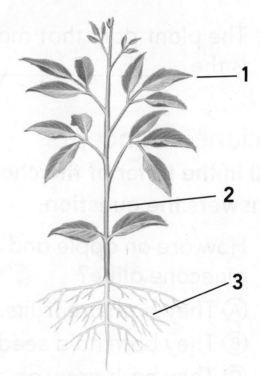

Ⓐ leaf
Ⓑ stem
Ⓒ roots

10. How are plants **different** from animals?

Ⓐ Plants need water and air.

Ⓑ Plants need space to grow.

Ⓒ Plants make their own food.

11. What kind of stems do shrubs have?

Ⓐ green stems

Ⓑ soft stems

Ⓒ woody stems

12. Read these steps for how a plant gets and uses water.

1. The roots take in water from the soil.

2. _____ ?

3. The leaves use water to make food.

Which step is missing?

Ⓐ The plant grows taller.

Ⓑ The flowers grow into fruit.

Ⓒ Water moves through the stem to all of the leaves.

Inquiry and the Big Idea
Write the answers to these questions.

13. Explain what each of these plant parts does.

   a. flowers

   _____

   b. fruits

   _____

   c. seeds

   _____

14. Look at this picture.

   a. How do you know that the plant is not meeting its basic needs?

   _____

   b. Name two things the plant needs.

   _____

© Houghton Mifflin Harcourt Publishing Company (c) ©Tom Tietz/Getty Images; (inset) ©Robert Pickett/Corbis; (border) ©NPS/Age Fotostock

UNIT 5
Environments

Big Idea

Environments can be found all over Earth. A living thing lives in an environment that meets its needs.

deer in the forest

I Wonder Why

Deer live in the forest. Why?
Turn the page to find out.

Here's Why A deer can meet its needs in the forest. It can find food, water, and shelter there.

In this unit, you will explore this Big Idea, the Essential Questions, and the Investigations on the Inquiry Flipchart.

Levels of Inquiry Key ■ DIRECTED ■ GUIDED ■ INDEPENDENT

Track Your Progress

Big Idea Environments can be found all over Earth. A living thing lives in an environment that meets its needs.

Essential Questions

Now I Get the Big Idea!

© Houghton Mifflin Harcourt Publishing Company   (t) ©Tom Tietz/Getty Images; (inset) ©Robert Pickett/Corbis; (border) ©NDisc/Age Fotostock

Science Notebook

Before you begin each lesson, be sure to write your thoughts about the Essential Question.

Essential Question

Where Do Plants and Animals Live?

 **Engage Your Brain!**

Find the answer to the question in the lesson.

What animal might live in this environment?

_____

_____

Active Reading

Lesson Vocabulary

1. Preview the lesson.

2. Write the 3 vocabulary terms here.

_____   _____

_____

All Around You

All the living and nonliving things around you make up your **environment**. A living thing lives in the environment that meets its needs.

Many animals need shelter. **Shelter** is a place where an animal can be safe.

Active Reading

Find the sentence that tells the meaning of **shelter**. Draw a line under the sentence.

The foxes are using this log for shelter.

Salty Water

An ocean environment is a large body of salt water. Its top layer is home to many living things. Here, plants and other living things get the sunlight they need. Animals can find food.

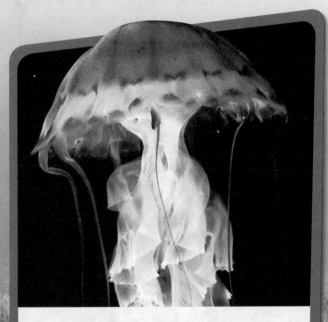

A jellyfish has body parts that help it catch its food.

Kelp lives in the ocean. Many animals eat it.

▶ Why do many plants live in the top layer of the ocean?

_____

_____

In a Rain Forest

A rain forest gets a lot of rain. The trees grow tall and block the sun. Many animals, such as birds and monkeys, use the tall trees for shelter. The shorter plants do not need much sunlight.

The rain forest provides everything this leopard needs to live.

▶ Draw a rain forest animal that might live in the trees.

Dry As a Bone

A desert environment gets little rain. Plants such as cactuses store water in their thick stems. Other plants store water in their leaves. In hot deserts, many animals hide during the day.

A Joshua tree can be a shelter for small animals.

Desert plants and animals can live with little water.

desert hare

Gila monster

▶**Draw a plant that stores water.**

It's Cold Out Here!

A tundra is a very cold environment.
Plants grow close together near the ground.
Animals have thick fur to stay warm.

An Arctic fox's white fur helps it hide in the snow.

Arctic flowers

▶ How does an Arctic fox's white fur help it in winter?

_____

_____

_____

On the Prairie

A prairie environment is mostly dry. It has just a few kinds of trees and shrubs. Large animals eat the tall grasses. Smaller animals live in the grasses.

Active Reading

The main idea is the most important idea about something. Draw two lines under the main idea.

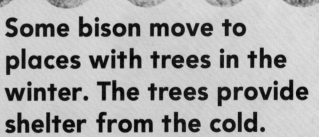

Some bison move to places with trees in the winter. The trees provide shelter from the cold.

coneflowers

prairie dogs

red-tailed hawk

The Food Chain

All living things need energy from the sun. Plants use sunlight to make food. Then animals eat the plants. They get the energy they need from the plants.

A **food chain** shows how energy moves from plants to animals.

The grass uses sunlight to make food.

► Trace the arrows to show the order of the food chain.

The cricket eats the grass.

The toad eats the cricket.

Do the Math!
Solve a Problem

Solve this problem.
A toad can eat about 40 crickets in 1 hour.

How many can it eat in 2 hours?

_____ crickets

Sum It Up!

① Draw It!

Choose an environment. Draw a living thing meeting its needs there.

② Order It!

Number the parts of the food chain to put them in order.

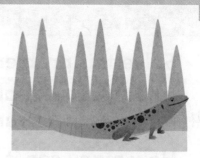

_____   _____   _____

Brain Check

Name _____

Word Play

Read the journal entry. Fill in the blanks using words from the box.

shelter	food chain	environment

Dear Journal,

Today I took a field trip to Mulberry Forest. It is an _____ full of trees. Birds use the trees for _____.

The trees need sunlight to make food. The birds eat berries from the trees. The sun, the trees, and the birds are part of a _____. It was fun to learn about the forest.

Your Friend,
Swati

Apply Concepts

Write two details that go with the main idea. Then answer the question.

Main Idea
A tundra is a cold environment.

Detail—Animals	Detail—Plants
_____	_____
_____	_____
_____	_____

What do all the living and nonliving things in a place make up? _____

Take It Home!

Family Members: Talk about your environment with your child. Look for examples of animals using plants for food and for shelter.

Ask a
Forest Ranger

What does a forest ranger do?
I take care of forests. I help keep plants and animals safe. I also teach about nature and how to care for it.

How does a forest ranger help keep plants safe?
I teach people how to keep forest fires from starting. I make sure no one cuts down trees.

How does a forest ranger help keep animals safe?
I make sure people do not feed them. I protect their homes by protecting the forest.

Now It's Your Turn!

▶ **What question would you ask a forest ranger?**

_____

_____

_____

Houghton Mifflin Harcourt Publishing Company (tg) ©Mike Dobel/Alamy; (inset) ©David Young-Wolff/Alamy

Protect the Forest

1

_____

_____

_____

▶ **Draw or write the answer to each question.**

1 Why are forest rangers important?

2

_____

_____

_____

2 What would you like best about being a forest ranger? What would you like least?

3 Suppose you are a forest ranger. Draw one animal or plant you help protect in the forest.

3

Name _____

Essential Question

What Is a Terrarium?

Set a Purpose

Tell what you want to find out.

_____

_____

Think About the Procedure

1 What do you put inside the bottle?

_____

_____

2 What will you observe about the pill bugs?

_____

_____

Record Your Data

Record what you observe in the chart.

My Pill Bug Observations	
Day 1	
Day 2	
Day 3	
Day 4	
Day 5	

Draw Conclusions

How did the terrarium help you understand what animals need to live?

_____

_____

Ask More Questions

What other questions could a terrarium help you answer?

_____

A Place for Animals

Keeping Animals Safe

People design and build safe places for animals. These places provide food, water, and shelter. People can help sick animals get well.

This animal doctor is checking on the health of the chimps.

These elephants are getting the food they need to live and grow.

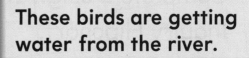

These birds are getting water from the river.

Map It!

This map shows a place designed for animals. People make sure the animals can meet their needs there. Use the map to find out how.

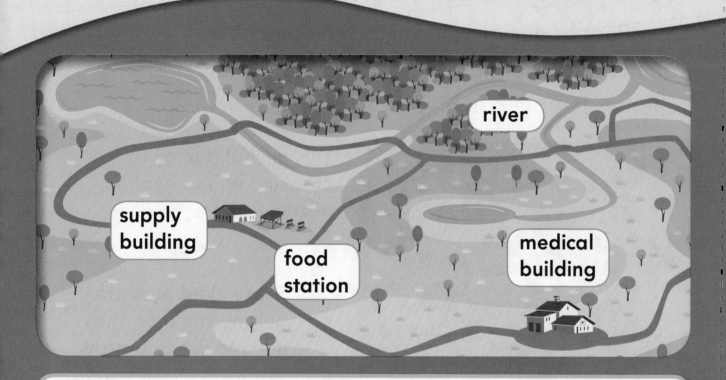

Circle where animals can get food.

Draw an X where animals can get water.

Draw a box around where sick animals can get well.

Build On It!

 Design a place for butterflies to live and grow. Complete **Design It: Butterfly Garden** on the Inquiry Flipchart.

Name _____

Vocabulary Review

Use the terms in the box to complete the sentences.

| environment |
| food chain |
| shelter |

1. A place where an animal can be safe is a _____.

2. All the living and nonliving things in a place make up an _____.

3. A path that shows how energy moves from plants to animals is called a _____.

Science Concepts

Fill in the letter of the choice that best answers the question.

4. Which words tell about a rain forest environment?
   Ⓐ dry and hot
   Ⓑ snowy and cold
   Ⓒ wet and shady

5. A kangaroo rat needs little water to live. It may eat seeds. Its shelter can be found underground. Which environment **best** meets its needs?
   Ⓐ a desert
   Ⓑ an ocean
   Ⓒ a tundra

6. This animal lives in the tundra.

How does its white fur help the animal stay alive?

Ⓐ It helps the animal hide in the snow.

Ⓑ It keeps the animal cool in summer.

Ⓒ It helps the animal store water.

7. Why do bison live on the prairie?

Ⓐ They like rainy environments.

Ⓑ They can meet their need for food by eating grass.

Ⓒ They are too big for any other environment.

8. You make a terrarium. You put in food, soil, plants, and some animals. What else do the animals need to survive?

Ⓐ rocks

Ⓑ twigs

Ⓒ water

9. How is this animal using the log?

Ⓐ for food

Ⓑ for shelter

Ⓒ for water

10. Arctic flowers grow well in cold, snowy places. They need little warmth. Where would they grow **best**?

Ⓐ a prairie

Ⓑ a rain forest

Ⓒ a tundra

11. Which of these living things might you find in an ocean environment?

Ⓐ a fish

Ⓑ a pine tree

Ⓒ a polar bear

12. What can you learn about this bird from the picture?

Ⓐ how old it is

Ⓑ what it eats

Ⓒ where it lives

Inquiry and the Big Idea
Write the answers to these questions.

13. Look at this picture.

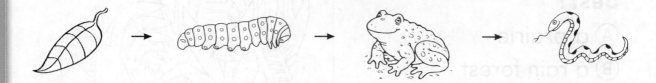

a. What does it show?

_____

b. How does the frog depend on the caterpillar to meet its basic needs?

_____

14. You put pill bugs in a jar with soil, damp leaves, and a few rotten vegetables. After a few days, you see that most of the vegetables are gone. You see pill bugs hiding under the damp leaves.

Describe two ways the environment helps the pill bugs meet their needs.

_____

_____

_____

UNIT 6
Earth's Resources

Big Idea

There are many kinds of resources on Earth.

sandy beach

I Wonder Why

Trash on the beach needs to be cleaned up. Why?
Turn the page to find out.

197

Here's Why Trash can be harmful to land, water, and living things at the beach.

In this unit, you will explore this Big Idea, the Essential Questions, and the Investigations on the Inquiry Flipchart.

Levels of Inquiry Key ■ DIRECTED ■ **GUIDED** ■ INDEPENDENT

Track Your Progress

Big Idea There are many kinds of resources on Earth.

Essential Questions

Now I Get the Big Idea!

Science Notebook

Before you begin each lesson, be sure to write your thoughts about the Essential Question.

Essential Question

What Can We Find on Earth?

🧠 Engage Your Brain!

Find the answer in the lesson.

The Great Sphinx was built long ago.

It was built from

_____.

Active Reading

Lesson Vocabulary

❶ Preview the lesson.

❷ Write the 3 vocabulary terms here.

_____   _____

_____

All Natural

What do you use from Earth? You use natural resources. A **natural resource** is anything from nature that people can use.

Air

Air is a natural resource. We breathe air. Wind is moving air. This hang glider uses wind to move. A wind farm changes wind into useful energy. Energy gives light and heat to homes.

Active Reading

Draw two lines under the main idea.

Water

Water is a natural resource.
We use water in many ways.

▶ Label each picture. Tell how people use water.

_____

_____   _____

Plants and Animals

Plants and animals are natural resources too. We use them for food. We also use them to make clothes and other things we need.

▶ **Look at the pictures. Circle the good we get from each plant or animal.**

We make socks from cotton.

We make wood toys from trees.

We make food from tomatoes.

202

We make a
sweater from a
sheep's wool.

We make cheese
from a cow's milk.

We get eggs
from a hen.

Rocks

Rocks are a natural resource. A **rock** is a hard nonliving object from the ground. We use rocks to build things.

Active Reading

Find the sentence that tells the meaning of **rock**. Draw a line under the sentence.

house made from rocks

Soil

Soil is a natural resource, too. **Soil** is the top layer of Earth. We use soil to grow plants. We can also use it to make things. We can use bricks for building.

▶ **How is this boy using soil?**

_____

_____

1 Write It!

Solve the riddle.

How are a , 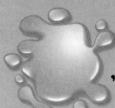, and a  alike?

They are all _____ .

2 Circle It!

Circle a way people use each natural resource.

Animal	Rock	Water	Soil

Name _____

Word Play

Write the resources on the lines.
Then color the picture.

1 What fruit comes from a plant? _____
Color it red.

2 What other resources are plants? _____
Color them green.

3 What resource is an animal? _____
Color it brown.

4 What resource do we drink? _____
Color it blue.

Apply Concepts

Fill in the organizer. Write the names of natural resources.

plants

Natural Resources

Take It Home!

Family Members: Work with your child to identify things in your home that are made from natural resources.

Learn About...

Dr. George Washington Carver

Dr. George Washington Carver was a scientist. He worked with farmers. Dr. Carver showed them how to plant peanuts to keep their soil good for growing crops.

Fun Fact

Dr. Carver invented peanut shampoo!

This Leads to That

Dr. George Washington Carver studied farming.

He taught farmers how to make their soil rich.

Today, farmers around the world use his ideas.

▶ **How did Dr. Carver help farmers?**

_____

_____

_____

Essential Question

What Are Rocks and Soil?

Engage Your Brain!

Find the answer to the question in the lesson.

How can people use soil?

to _____

Active Reading

Lesson Vocabulary

❶ Preview the lesson.

❷ Write the 2 vocabulary terms here.

_____ _____

Ready to Rock

Rocks are hard, nonliving objects from the ground. Rocks may be different colors and shapes. Rocks may be big or small. Color, shape, and size are properties of rocks. A **property** is one part of what something is like.

Active Reading

Find the sentence that tells the meaning of **property**. Draw a line under the sentence.

Properties of Rocks

▶ **Circle the names of three properties of rocks.**

Color Rocks may be different colors.

Shape Rocks may be different shapes.

Size Rocks may be different sizes.

Super Soil

Soil is made up of small pieces of rock and once-living things. It forms a layer on parts of Earth's surface. Soil is an important resource. We use soil to grow plants.

Active Reading

A detail is a fact that tells about a main idea. Draw one line under a detail. Draw an arrow to the main idea the detail tells about.

© Houghton Mifflin Harcourt Publishing Company (bg) ©Digital Vision/Getty Images

How Soil Forms

Wind and water break down rock. Bits of rock form the base of soil.

Dead plants and animals fall to the ground. They break down into bits. These bits mix with the bits of broken rock.

▶ Trace the dashed lines to show how soil forms.

The Scoop on Soil

Soils may be different. Soils may have different colors and textures. **Texture** is what an object feels like. Color and texture are two properties of soil.

Some soils are better than others for growing plants.

Properties of Soil

Color The color of soil comes from the rocks and other things found in it.

Texture The size and shape of the rock bits make different textures. Once-living things make different textures, too.

▶ **Circle the black soil. Draw an X on the roughest soil.**

Sum It Up!

1 Circle It!

Circle the sentence that is <u>true</u>.

All soils have the same texture.

Soils can be different colors.

2 Order It!

Write 1, 2, 3 to order how a plant becomes part of soil.

_____ The plant breaks down into bits.

_____ A dead plant falls to the ground.

_____ The bits become part of soil.

3 Draw It!

Draw a rock that has the properties in the box.

gray   large   round

218

Word Play

Draw a line through the maze to match each word with its meaning.

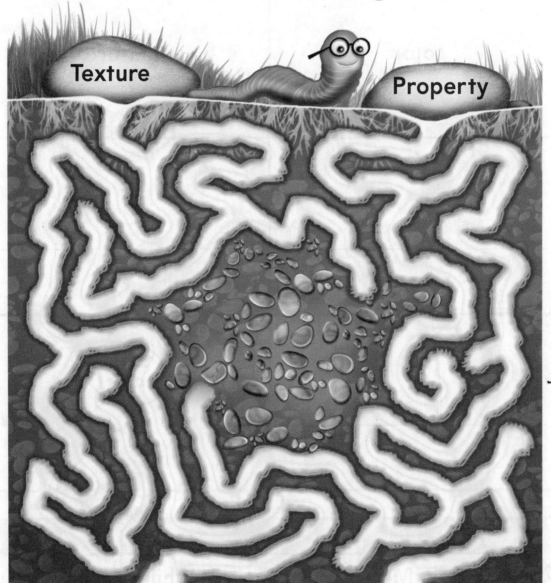

Texture

Property

is what an object feels like.

is one part of what something is like.

Apply Concepts

Name the properties of rocks and soil.

Properties of Rocks and Soil

Rocks	Soil
color	texture
_____	_____
_____	You rock!

Family Members: With your child, observe soil outside or in a potted plant. Have your child name some properties of soil.

Take It Home!

Name _____

What Can We Observe About Rocks?

Set a Purpose
Tell what you want to find out.

_____

_____

Think About the Procedure
❶ What do you find out when you observe the rocks?

_____

_____

❷ What are some ways you can sort rocks?

_____

Record Your Data

Draw or write about how you sorted the rocks.

Ways I Sorted		

Draw Conclusions

How can rocks be alike and different?

_____

_____

_____

Ask More Questions

What other things about rocks could you test?

_____

_____

Name _____

Essential Question

How Do Soils Differ?

Set a Purpose

Tell what you want to find out.

_____

Think About the Procedure

1 How many soil samples will you compare?

_____

2 Name some properties of soil that you will observe.

_____

_____

_____

Record Your Data

Draw and write to record what you observe.

Property	Soil Sample 1	Soil Sample 2
Color		
Texture		
Size and Shape of Bits		
Living or Once-living Things		

Draw Conclusions

How are the soils the same? How are they different?

_____

_____

_____

Ask More Questions

What other questions could you ask about soil?

_____

© Houghton Mifflin Harcourt Publishing Company

Essential Question

Where Can We Find Water?

Engage Your Brain!

Find the answer to the question in the lesson.

How much of Earth is covered with water?

_____

Active Reading

Lesson Vocabulary

1. Preview the lesson.

2. Write the 4 vocabulary terms here.

_____   _____

_____   _____

So Fresh

Most plants and animals need fresh water. People need fresh water too. Fresh water is not salty. You can find fresh water in many places.

Streams

A **stream** is a small body of flowing water.

Rivers

Some streams flow into rivers. A **river** is a large body of flowing water.

► **How are lakes different from streams and rivers?**

_____

_____

Lakes

A **lake** is a body of water with land all around it. Water in a lake does not flow.

So Salty

You can find water in oceans too.
An **ocean** is a large body of salty water.
Most of Earth's water is in oceans.

Active Reading

A detail is a fact about a main idea. Draw one line under a detail. Draw an arrow to the main idea it tells about.

surfer in ocean

Do the Math!
Model Fractions

About $\frac{3}{4}$, or three fourths, of Earth is covered with water. The rest is covered with land.

This circle models Earth's water and land. It has 4 parts. Color the parts to show how much water is on Earth.

Now look at the circle. How much of Earth is covered with land?

Answer: _____

Wonderful Water

All living things need water. Plants, animals, and people need it to stay healthy.

People drink water.

Animals drink water.

Save Earth's water!

Water flows through this dam.

We must protect water and keep it clean.

Follow these tips to help.

1 Use less water for baths and showers.

2 Fix leaky pipes or faucets.

3 Put trash in trash cans! Do not put trash in water.

▶ **Add your own tip for protecting Earth's water.**

_____

_____

_____

Plants need water too.

Jump into Safety!

Water Safety

- Learn to swim.
- Never swim alone.
- Watch the weather.
- Wear a life jacket on a boat.
- Do not dive in shallow water.
- Call 911 if there is an emergency.

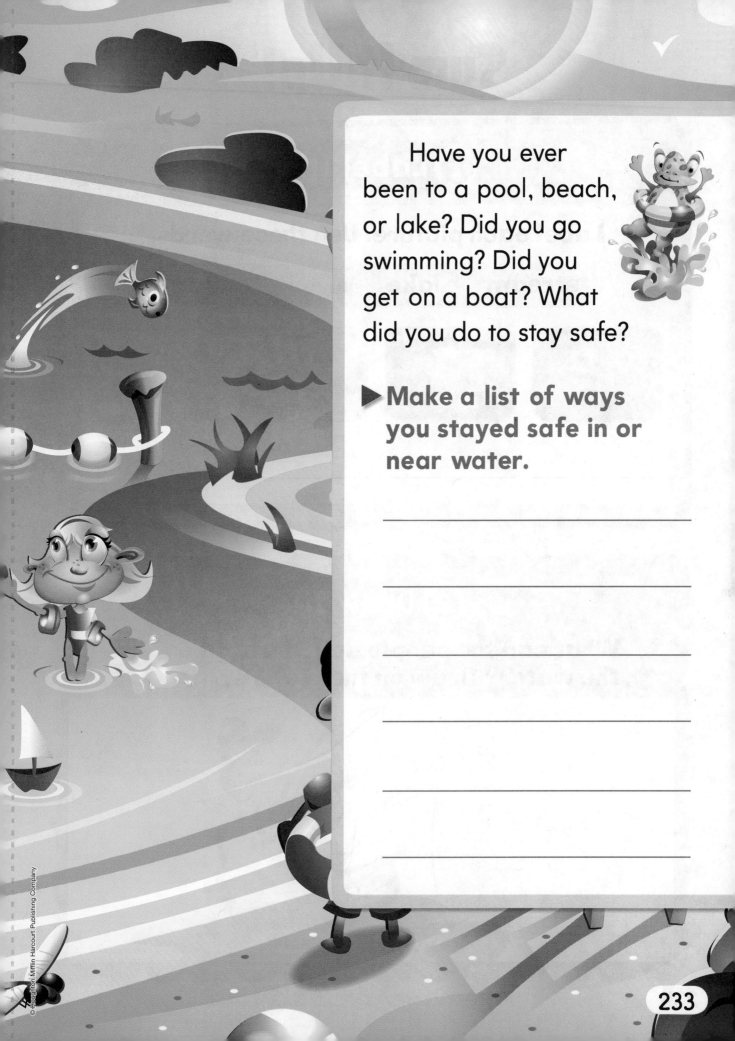

Have you ever been to a pool, beach, or lake? Did you go swimming? Did you get on a boat? What did you do to stay safe?

▶ Make a list of ways you stayed safe in or near water.

_____

_____

_____

_____

_____

Sum It Up!

1 Label It!

Label each picture. Use these words.

stream   lake   river   ocean

_____   _____   _____   _____

2 Draw It!

What can the people do to be safe on the water? Draw on the picture.

Word Play

Name _____

Fill in the blanks. Use these words.

ocean	lake	stream	river	fresh water

Most lakes have __ __ __ __ __ ◯ __ __ __ __ .

An __ __ __ ◯ __ has salty water.

A __ ◯ __ __ __ __ is a small body of water.

A __ __ __ ◯ has water that does not flow.

Streams can flow together to
make a ◯ __ __ __ __ .

**Then use the circled letters
to fill in the blanks below.**

We use __ __ __ __ __ in
many ways!

Apply Concepts

Write your answer to each question.

1 Why do we need water?

_____

_____

_____

2 How can we stay safe around water?

- _____

- _____

- _____

- _____

Take It Home!

Family Members: Work with your child to identify ways to save water at home.

Essential Question

How Can We Save Resources?

🧠 Engage Your Brain!

Find the answer to the question in the lesson.

This art uses old things to make something new. How does this help Earth?

It makes less

_____ .

Active Reading

Lesson Vocabulary

❶ Preview the lesson.

❷ Write the 4 vocabulary terms here.

_____   _____

_____   _____

What a Waste!

Pollution is waste that harms land, water, and air. It can make people and animals sick. Plants can be harmed, too. Pollution makes water unsafe to drink. It also makes the air dirty. Dirty air is unsafe to breathe. We all need clean resources.

Active Reading

Find the sentence that tells the meaning of **pollution**. Draw a line under the sentence.

Draw a circle on the air pollution.
Draw an X on the land pollution.
Draw a box on the water pollution.

Pollution Solutions

People can help keep land, water, and air clean. They can put trash in trash cans. People can keep waste away from water. They can drive less to help keep the air clean. Planting trees can clean the air, too.

▶ **Look at the pictures in each row. Write land, water, or air to complete each sentence.**

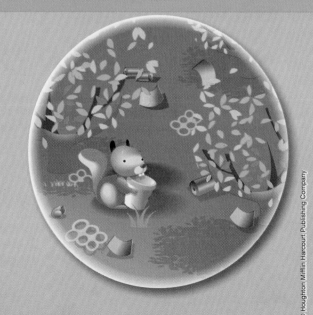

240

**People ride bikes.
This keeps the
_____ clean.**

**People keep waste
out of the river.
This keeps the
_____ clean.**

**People put trash in
cans. This keeps the
_____ clean.**

Care for Earth!

You care for resources when you use less of them. You can reduce, reuse, and recycle. This makes less trash.

To **reduce** is to use less of something. You use less water when you turn the faucet off. To **reuse** is to use something again. You can reuse a can to make a pencil holder. To **recycle** is to use old things to make new things. You can recycle the plastic in bottles to make something new.

Active Reading

An effect tells what happens. Draw two lines under an effect of **reducing**, **reusing**, and **recycling**.

▶ Tell about the picture. Write
reduce, reuse, or recycle.

_____ _____ _____

_____

_____

Good As New

Have you ever worn a shirt made from plastic bottles? You may have! We can recycle and reuse many old things. Metal from cans may be recycled to make a new baseball bat. A metal can may also be reused as a planter. Paper can be reused and recycled, too.

▶ **Match each object on the left to what it became on the right.**

1 milk jug

2 newspaper

3 cans

◯—

playground equipment

◯—

paper crane

◯—

bat

Do the Math!

Solve a Word Problem

Solve the problem.

5 plastic bottles make 1 shirt.

How many shirts do 10 plastic bottles make?

_____ shirts

① Draw It!

Draw a picture of land pollution.
Draw a picture of water pollution.

land

water

② Match It!

Draw a line to match each word to the picture it tells about.

recycle

reduce

reuse

Name _____

Word Play

Write words from the box to complete the letter.

| pollution | reduce | reuse | recycle |

Dear Ben,

    I just joined a club. We _____ paper so it can be made into new things. We _____ cans to make pencil holders. It is a good idea to shut off lights when we leave rooms. This helps _____ our use of resources.

    Soon we will clean up trash in the park. _____ could harm the living things there. Let's go to the park together!

Your Friend,
Ming

Apply Concepts

Write a word from the box to fill in the blanks.

| reduce | reuse | recycle |

Cause

Effect

I _____
a bottle as a
flower vase.

➡️ I make less trash.

I _____ cans.

➡️ The old cans are
used to make
new pots.

I turn off the
water when I
brush my teeth.

➡️ I _____
the amount of
water I use.

Changing Cars

Building a Better Car

Most cars run on gas. These cars make air pollution. Engineers are making new cars that are better for the air.

A hybrid car runs on gas and electricity. It makes less pollution than a car that runs only on gas.

An electric car runs on electricity. It does not make any pollution at all!

gas car

hybrid car

electric car

Electric cars run for only a short time. Engineers are working on this problem.

Which Car Is Best?

Read the sentences below.
Then answer the questions.

You want to take a short car trip. You do not want to make any pollution. Which car would you choose to take your trip? Why?

_____

_____

_____

_____

Build On It!

 Solve a problem about air pollution. Complete **Solve It: Use Fewer Cars** on the Inquiry Flipchart.

Name _____

Vocabulary Review

Use the terms in the box to complete the sentences.

natural
resource
pollution
texture

1. Anything from nature that people can use is a _____.

2. Waste that harms land, water, and air is called _____.

3. The way an object feels is its _____.

Science Concepts

Fill in the letter of the choice that best answers the question.

4. Which natural resource do people use to drink?
   Ⓐ air
   Ⓑ soil
   Ⓒ water

5. Which is **true** of a river?
   Ⓐ It has land on all sides.
   Ⓑ It may flow into an ocean.
   Ⓒ It does not have fresh water.

6. Aisha sorted these rocks into two groups.

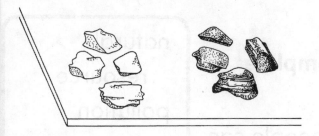

Which property did she use to sort them?

Ⓐ color

Ⓑ shape

Ⓒ size

7. Why are soils different colors?

Ⓐ They get different amounts of rain.

Ⓑ They have different materials in them.

Ⓒ They hold different amounts of water.

8. The Yuans ride their bikes whenever they can. What natural resource do they protect?

Ⓐ air

Ⓑ rocks

Ⓒ water

9. Which water safety rule are the people breaking?

Ⓐ Learn to swim.

Ⓑ Never swim alone.

Ⓒ Wear a life jacket when boating.

10. What makes up soil?
   Ⓐ only once-living things
   Ⓑ only rocks and water
   Ⓒ once-living things and rocks

11. Which body of water has land all around it?
   Ⓐ lake
   Ⓑ river
   Ⓒ stream

12. This bird feeder is made from a milk carton.

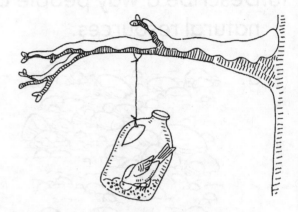

Which word describes how the milk carton is being used?

   Ⓐ recycle
   Ⓑ reduce
   Ⓒ reuse

Inquiry and the Big Idea
Write the answers to these questions.

13. Describe a way people can use each of these natural resources.

a.

_____

b.

_____

14. Describe how you can reuse something at home or at school. How does reusing things help the environment?

_____

_____

_____

UNIT 7

Weather and Seasons

winter weather

Big Idea

Weather changes from day to day and from season to season. You can use different tools to measure weather.

I Wonder Why

Icicles form in winter. Why?

Turn the page to find out.

Here's Why Air in the winter is cold. Cold air causes liquid water to freeze into a solid.

In this unit, you will explore this Big Idea, the Essential Questions, and the Investigations on the Inquiry Flipchart.

Levels of Inquiry Key ■ DIRECTED ■ GUIDED ■ INDEPENDENT

Track Your Progress

Big Idea Weather changes from day to day and from season to season. You can use different tools to measure weather.

Essential Questions

Now I Get the Big Idea!

Science Notebook

Before you begin each lesson, be sure to write your thoughts about the Essential Question.

Essential Question
What Is Weather?

Engage Your Brain!

Find the answer to the question in the lesson.

Rainbows usually follow rainy weather. Which tool could you use to measure rainfall?

_____

Active Reading

Lesson Vocabulary
1 Preview the lesson.

2 Write the 3 vocabulary terms here.

_____   _____

_____

Weather Watch

Look outside. Is the sun out? Is the air warm or cool? Are there any clouds? Do you feel any wind? **Wind** is air that moves.

Weather is what the air outside is like. Weather may change during the day. It may also change from day to day and from month to month.

Active Reading

A detail is a fact about a main idea. Draw one line under a detail. Draw an arrow to the main idea the detail tells about.

Is it cloudy or sunny?

Is it windy or calm?

Is it rainy or icy?

Is it hot or cold?

Is it cloudy or clear?

▶ **Circle the word that tells about the weather in each picture.**

Measure It!

You can use tools to measure weather. A thermometer is a tool that measures temperature. **Temperature** is the measure of how hot or cold something is. Temperature is measured in degrees.

Active Reading

Find the sentence that tells the meaning of **temperature**. Draw a line under the sentence.

thermometer

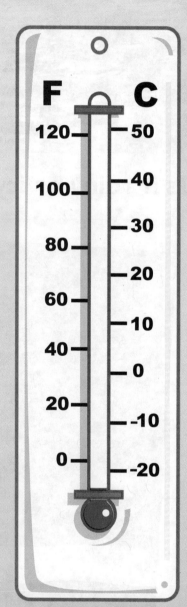

▶ **Color the thermometer to show 80 °F.**

Rain, snow, sleet, and hail are
forms of water that fall from the sky.
A rain gauge is a tool that measures
how much water falls.

rain gauge

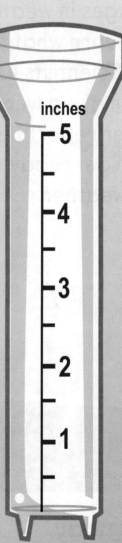

▶ **Color the rain gauge to show
that 3 inches of rain fell.**

Predict It!

Scientists observe and track weather over time. They look for changes in weather. They use tools to learn what the weather may be. Scientists use what they learn to make a weather report. A weather report helps people. They can get ready for the coming weather.

weather satellite

Do the Math!
Compare Numbers

Monday	Tuesday	Wednesday

50 °F	40 °F	45 °F

We use these tools to observe and track weather.

weather station

weather balloon

Look at the temperatures on the left.

Write one of them in the empty box below.

Write >, <, or = to compare the two numbers.

| 45 °F | | _____ °F |

Sum It Up!

① Draw It!

Draw a picture to show cloudy and windy weather.

② Solve It!

Write a weather word to solve.

You may see me in a puddle outside.
The day is gray when I fall from the sky.

I am _____.

③ Match It!

Match the words to the pictures.

   rain gauge

   thermometer

Name _____

Word Play

Write a word from the box for each clue.

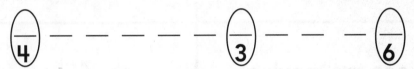

| wind | thermometer | temperature |

a measure of how hot or cold something is

$\left(\dfrac{\ \ }{4}\right)$ — — — — $\left(\dfrac{\ \ }{3}\right)$ — — — $\left(\dfrac{\ \ }{6}\right)$

air that is moving

$\left(\dfrac{\ \ }{1}\right)$ — — —

a tool used to measure temperature

— $\left(\dfrac{\ \ }{5}\right)$ — — — — $\left(\dfrac{\ \ }{2}\right)$ — — $\left(\dfrac{\ \ }{7}\right)$

Solve the riddle. Write the circled letters in order on the lines below.

I am what the air outside is like.
What am I?

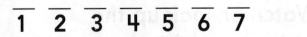

$\overline{1}\ \ \overline{2}\ \ \overline{3}\ \ \overline{4}\ \ \overline{5}\ \ \overline{6}\ \ \overline{7}$

Apply Concepts

Write a word from the box to fill in the blanks.

cold	windy	sunny	hot

Observation	Inference
Children are swimming in the lake.	The day is _hot_.
The trees are moving back and forth.	The day is _windy_.
People are wearing warm coats.	The day is _____.
People are wearing sunglasses.	The day is _____.

Take It Home!

Family Members: Watch or look up the weather forecast with your child. Have your child choose the right clothing for the weather.

wind ↗
wind ↗

Name _____

Essential Question

What Can We Observe About Weather?

Set a Purpose
Tell what you want to find out.

_____

_____

Think About the Procedure
❶ When will you observe the weather?

_____

_____

❷ What will you observe?

_____

_____

Record Your Data

Glue picture cards into the chart to show the weather.

Weather This Week

Monday	Tuesday	Wednesday	Thursday	Friday

Draw Conclusions

How is the weather alike from day to day?
How is the weather different from day to day?

_____

_____

How did you make your prediction?

_____

Ask More Questions

What other questions could you ask about the weather?

_____

268

Picture Cards

Cut out the weather cards on the dashed lines.

clear	clear	clear	clear	clear
cloudy	cloudy	cloudy	cloudy	cloudy
rainy	rainy	rainy	rainy	rainy
icy	icy	icy	icy	icy
hot	hot	hot	hot	hot
cold	cold	cold	cold	cold
windy	windy	windy	windy	windy

© Houghton Mifflin Harcourt Publishing Company

269

4 Things to Know About
June Bacon-Bercey

1 June Bacon-Bercey is a meteorologist.

2 She was the first female meteorologist on television.

3 She won money, which she used to help other women become meteorologists.

4 She enjoys teaching.

Word Whiz

▶ Learn weather words. Find the words in the word search below. Draw a circle around each word you find.

tornado   hurricane   lightning   thunder   storm   blizzard

l i g h t n i n g q
w m r n o t b y v h
b d l z r x s p c u
t t h u n d e r b r
i j g s a y z q m r
z q f g d g f d s i
z w s t o r m h j c
a r d k y y p l k a
r t s h p q w r t n
d y p f j s d c b e

Essential Question

What Are Seasons?

Engage Your Brain!

Find the answer to the question in the lesson.

In which season do many trees have no leaves?

_____

Active Reading

Lesson Vocabulary

1 Preview the lesson.

2 Write the 2 vocabulary terms here.

_____   _____

Spring Into Spring

A **season** is a time of year. Spring, summer, fall, and winter are the four seasons. They form a repeating pattern.

The weather changes with each season. These changes form a weather pattern. A **weather pattern** is a change in the weather that repeats.

Active Reading

Find the sentence that tells the meaning of **season**. Draw a line under the sentence.

People plant flowers in spring.

In spring, the air warms. There may be many rainy days. Plants begin to grow. Trees grow new leaves. People can wear light jackets outside.

▶ Circle the adult that has its young in spring.

Some animals have their young in spring.

Sunny Summer

Summer is the season that follows spring. In summer, the air can be hot. Some places may have storms. There are more hours of daylight than in spring.

Some plants grow fruit in summer. Young animals grow bigger. People dress to stay cool. They wear hats and sunglasses to keep safe from the sun.

▶ **Draw an object on the adult that would keep him safe from the sun.**

People canoe in summer.

▶ **Draw to show how most trees look in summer.**

This hare's fur is brown in summer. The brown fur helps the hare hide.

Fall Into Fall

Fall is the season that follows summer. The air gets cooler. There are fewer hours of daylight than in summer.

Some leaves change color and drop off the trees. Some animals move to warmer places. People wear jackets to stay warm.

Active Reading

A detail is a fact about a main idea. Draw one line under a detail. Draw an arrow to the main idea it tells about.

People rake leaves in fall.

▶ Draw to show how some trees look in fall.

Some animals gather food to store in winter.

Winter Weather

Winter is the season that follows fall. In some places, the air can be cold. It may even snow. Winter has the fewest hours of daylight.

Many trees lose their leaves in winter. Some animals grow more fur to keep warm. People wear warm coats outside. In a few months, it will be spring again.

▶ **Draw winter clothes on the person not dressed for the season.**

People play in the snow in winter.

► Draw to show how most trees look in winter.

The hare's fur has turned white. The hare can hide in the snow.

Sum It Up!

① Solve It!

Write the word that solves the riddle.

I am a time when trees have lots of leaves, or no leaves at all.

I am winter, spring, summer, or fall.

I am a _____ .

② Draw It!

Draw an activity you can do in spring.

③ Match It!

Match each word to the picture it tells about.

summer

winter

fall

Name _____

Word Play

Use the words below to complete the puzzle.

season	weather pattern	winter
spring	summer	fall

Across

1. the season that follows fall

2. the season that follows spring

3. the season that follows summer

4. a time of year

Down

5. the season that follows winter

6. a change in the weather that repeats

Apply Concepts

Cross out the things that do <u>not</u> belong in each picture.

Family Members: Plan out family activities for the four seasons. Discuss with your child how the weather affects what you do and what you wear.

Take It Home!

Weather Wisdom

Weather Tools

People use many tools to observe and record weather. The tools have changed over time. Weather vanes are older tools. Weather satellites are newer tools.

A thermometer measures temperature.

A weather satellite records weather from space.

A weather vane tells the direction of the wind.

A weather plane records weather from the sky.

Weather Tool Timeline

Use the timeline to answer the questions.

1. Which is the oldest weather tool? Circle it.

2. Which is the newest weather tool? Draw a box around it.

3. Which tool came after the thermometer? Draw an X over it.

Build On It!

Design and build your own rain gauge. Complete **Build It: Rain Gauge** on the Inquiry Flipchart.

Name _____

Vocabulary Review

Use the terms in the box to complete the sentences.

season
weather
 pattern
weather

1. What the air outside is like is called _____.

2. A time of year is a _____.

3. A change in the weather that repeats is a _____.

Science Concepts

Fill in the letter of the choice that best answers the question.

4. What tool do you use to record the temperature each day?
   Ⓐ a rain gauge
   Ⓑ a thermometer
   Ⓒ a weather vane

5. You see dark clouds in the sky. What kind of weather is **most likely** coming?
   Ⓐ cold weather
   Ⓑ rainy weather
   Ⓒ sunny weather

6. In which season was this young lamb born?

Ⓐ fall
Ⓑ spring
Ⓒ summer

7. The Han family is ice skating outside. They are wearing heavy jackets. What season is it?

Ⓐ spring
Ⓑ summer
Ⓒ winter

8. How is fall **different** from spring?

Ⓐ Fall is a season.
Ⓑ People may wear jackets in spring.
Ⓒ Many trees lose their leaves in fall.

9. What does a rain gauge measure?

Ⓐ the direction of the wind
Ⓑ how much rain has fallen
Ⓒ the temperature of the air

10. Look at this picture. What is the weather like?

Ⓐ clear and cold
Ⓑ cold and snowy
Ⓒ windy and warm

11. What is wind?
Ⓐ moving air
Ⓑ water from the sky
Ⓒ a tool for measuring temperature

12. Look at what the children are doing.

Which season is it?
Ⓐ fall
Ⓑ spring
Ⓒ summer

Inquiry and the Big Idea
Write the answers to these questions.

13. Look at the picture.

   a. What is the weather like?

   _____

   b. What might you wear on a day like this?

   _____

   c. What might you do on a day like this?

   _____

14. Look at the tree.

   a. What season is it? How do you know?

   _____

   _____

   b. Which season comes next?

   _____

Objects in the Sky

moon in the nighttime sky

Big Idea

The sun warms land, air, and water. The appearance of objects in the sky changes.

I Wonder Why

The moon looks lit in the nighttime sky. Why?
Turn the page to find out.

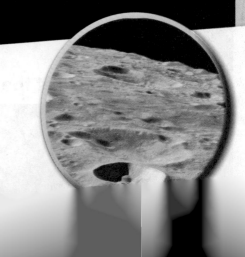

Here's Why The moon reflects light from the sun. This makes it look lit at nighttime.

In this unit, you will explore this Big Idea, the Essential Questions, and the Investigations on the Inquiry Flipchart.

Levels of Inquiry Key ■ DIRECTED ■ **GUIDED** ■ INDEPENDENT

Track Your Progress

Big Idea The sun warms land, air, and water. The appearance of objects in the sky changes.

Essential Questions

Now I Get the Big Idea!

Science Notebook

Before you begin each lesson, be sure to write your thoughts about the Essential Question.

Essential Question

What Can We See in the Sky?

Engage Your Brain!

Find the answer to the question in the lesson.

When can you see the moon?

_____

Active Reading

Lesson Vocabulary

1 Preview the lesson.

2 Write the 5 vocabulary terms here.

_____   _____

_____   _____

_____

Good Morning, Sunshine

sun

Look up! You can see many things in the daytime sky. You can see the sun. The **sun** is the star closest to Earth. A **star** is an object in the sky. It gives off its own light. The sun gives light and heat to Earth.

You may also see clouds in the daytime sky. Sometimes, you can even see the moon.

Active Reading

The main idea is the most important idea about something. Draw two lines under the main idea.

clouds

▶ **What can you see in the daytime sky? Look out your window. Draw what you see.**

Good Night, Sky

moon

You can see many things in the nighttime sky. You may see the moon. The **moon** is a large sphere, or ball of rock. It does not give off its own light. You may also see clouds at night.

Active Reading

Draw one line under a detail. Draw an arrow to the main idea it tells about.

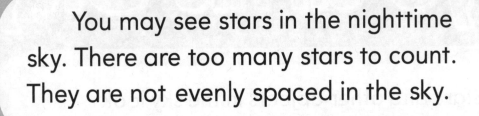

You may see stars in the nighttime sky. There are too many stars to count. They are not evenly spaced in the sky.

star

Do the Math!

Compare Solid Shapes

Many objects in the sky are spheres. A sphere is a round ball. The moon is a sphere. So is the sun. Color the spheres below.

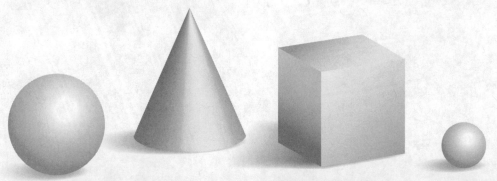

Eye on the Sky

Stars and other objects in the sky look small. We can magnify them to see them better. **Magnify** means to make something look bigger. A **telescope** is a tool that helps us magnify things in the sky.

▶ **Which picture shows the moon through a telescope? Mark an X on it.**

telescope

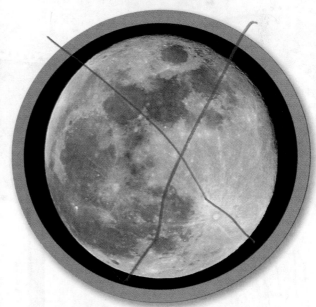

Both pictures show the moon.

Sum It Up!

① Solve It!

Solve the riddle.

I am a tool. I make things look bigger. You can use me to observe things in the sky.

What am I?

_____

② Circle It!

Circle <u>true</u> or <u>false</u>.

Stars are evenly spaced in the sky.

true   false

Stars give off their own light.

true   false

③ Draw It!

Draw what you can see in the sky at both times.

daytime	nighttime

Name _____

Word Play

Unscramble the letters to complete each sentence.

sun   star   telescope   magnify   moon

omon   The ___ ___ ___ ___ is a large ball
            of rock.

tasr   A ___ ___ ___ ___ gives off its
            own light.

eletopsce   A ___ ___ ___ ___ ___ ___ ___ ___ ___
            is a tool for making things
            look bigger.

usn   The ___ ___ ___ is the star we see
            in the day.

fimgany   To ___ ___ ___ ___ ___ ___ ___ is to
            make things look bigger.

Apply Concepts

1 Fill in the diagram to compare.
Use the words below.

| sun | stars | clouds | moon |

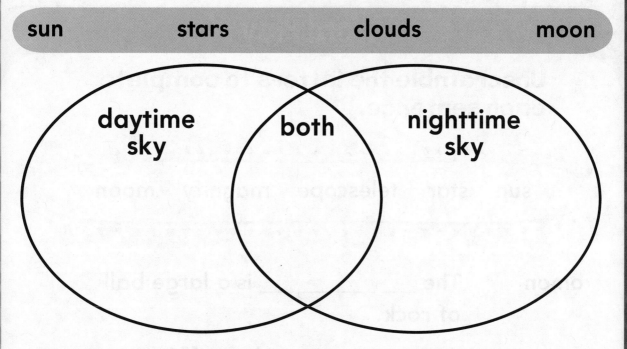

daytime
sky

both

nighttime
sky

2 Draw a nighttime sky full of stars.

Take It Home!

Family Members: Observe the nighttime sky
with your child. Have your child explain how
it looks different from the daytime sky.

302

4

Things to Know About

Galileo Galilei

1 Galileo lived in Italy more than 400 years ago.

2 His telescope made objects look 20 times bigger.

3 He discovered sunspots on the sun.

4 He found out that the planet Jupiter has four moons.

This Leads to That

Galileo used his telescope to observe the sun and planets.

He proved that Earth moves around the sun.

▶ **People used to think that the sun moved around Earth. Galileo proved this was wrong. Why is this important?**

_____

_____

_____

Essential Question

How Does the Sky Seem to Change?

Engage Your Brain!

Find the answer to the question in the lesson.

Why does the sun seem to move across the sky?

Earth _____ .

Active Reading

Lesson Vocabulary

❶ Preview the lesson.

❷ Write the 2 vocabulary terms here.

_____ _____

Hello, Shadow

The sun is the brightest object in the daytime sky. It warms Earth's land, air, and water. The sun seems to move across the sky. But the sun is not moving. It is really Earth that is moving. Each day, Earth turns all the way around.

Active Reading

The main idea is the most important idea about something. Draw two lines under the main idea.

morning

Light from the sun makes shadows. A **shadow** is a dark place made where an object blocks light. Shadows change as Earth moves. The sun's light shines on objects from different directions as the day goes on. Shadows change in size during the day. They change position, too.

▶ **At what time of day is the girl's shadow the shortest?**

_____

noon

afternoon

Just a Phase

Now it is night. You may see stars. You may see the moon. The moon is a huge ball of rock. It does not give off its own light. The moon reflects light from the sun.

Active Reading

A detail is a fact about a main idea. Draw one line under a detail. Draw an arrow to the main idea it tells about.

new moon

first quarter moon

The moon moves across the sky. Its shape seems to change. The **phases**, or shapes you see, change as the moon moves. The changes follow a repeating pattern. It lasts about a month.

▶ Today there is a full moon. Write what the moon's phase will be in about a month.

_____

full moon

third quarter moon

Cloudy Day, Starry Night

You can see stars in the nighttime sky. Stars give off light. You see different stars in each season.

You can see clouds in both the daytime and nighttime sky. Clouds change shape from day to day.

You may see these stars in summer.

You may see these stars in winter.

**These kinds
of clouds may
bring rain.**

**These kinds of
clouds can be seen
on a sunny day.**

▶ **Draw a cloud that
might bring rain.**

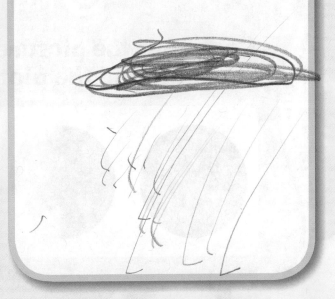

Sum It Up!

① Solve It!

Write the word to solve the riddle.

I am fluffy or thin.
I am white or gray.
I come out on
some days and then
go away.
I am a _____.

② Draw It!

Draw the boy's shadow in the morning.

③ Mark It!

Cross out the picture of the full moon. Put a box around the picture of the new moon.

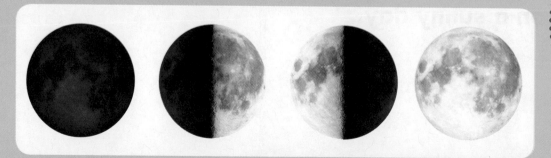

Brain Check

Name _____

Word Play

Label each picture with a word from the box.
Match the word to its meaning.

| sun | phases | shadow |

dark place made where an object blocks light

_____

shapes you see of the moon

_____

brightest object in the daytime sky

_____

Apply Concepts

Write the words that tell more about each column. Each word may be used more than once.

| sun | clouds | stars | moon |

Daytime Sky	Nighttime Sky	Gives Off Its Own Light	Moves or Seems to Move
_____	_____	_____	_____
_____	_____	_____	_____
_____	_____		_____
			_____

Take It Home! **Family Members:** Look at the moon with your child for a few nights in a row. Ask your child to describe how the moon seems to change shape.

Name _____

Essential Question

How Does the Sun Seem to Move?

Set a Purpose
Tell what you want to find out.

_____

_____

Think About the Procedure

1 When will you look at your shadow?

_____

_____

2 How will you know how your shadow changes?

_____

Record Your Data

Write the number of shoes in the chart.

My Shadow's Length

Morning	Noon	Afternoon
_____ shoes long	_____ shoes long	_____ shoes long

Draw Conclusions

How did your shadow change from morning to noon?

_____

How did it change from noon to afternoon?

_____

Why do you think your shadow changed?

_____

_____

Ask More Questions

What other questions could you ask about shadows?

_____

_____

316

See the Light

Compare Flashlights

Lights help you see what you are doing. They help you get around at night. The lights in a building make it bright.

Flashlights can light up dark places. Flashlights work in different ways.

- uses a switch
- needs batteries
- lights up right away

- uses a hand crank
- does not need batteries
- takes time to light up

Bright Ideas

Think about a kind of light, like a lamp.
How can you make it better? Draw your
design. Tell how your design works.

Build On It!

 Design lights for a ballpark. Complete **Design It:
Lights for a Park** on the Inquiry Flipchart.

Unit 8 Review

Vocabulary Review

Use the terms in the box to complete the sentences.

| phases |
| shadow |
| star |

1. An object in the sky that gives off its own light is a

   _____.

2. A dark place made where an object blocks light is a

   _____.

3. The shapes of the moon you see as it moves are its

   _____.

Science Concepts

Fill in the letter of the choice that best answers the question.

4. How many stars are in the sky?
   Ⓐ about 20
   Ⓑ not enough to be counted
   Ⓒ more than anyone can easily count

5. What objects can we see in the nighttime sky?
   Ⓐ the sun and clouds
   Ⓑ the moon and stars
   Ⓒ the sun and the moon

6. What heats Earth's land, water, and air?
   Ⓐ clouds
   Ⓑ the moon
   Ⓒ the sun

7. What moon phase does this picture show?

   Ⓐ full moon
   Ⓑ new moon
   Ⓒ first quarter moon

8. Which happens because Earth turns?
   Ⓐ The sun warms Earth.
   Ⓑ The moon has phases.
   Ⓒ The sun seems to move across the sky.

9. How do stars look in the nighttime sky?
   Ⓐ They are scattered unevenly.
   Ⓑ They are set in a pattern of rings.
   Ⓒ They are set evenly across the sky.

10. Which picture shows the flag at the end of the day?

Ⓐ The picture with the long shadow.

Ⓑ The picture with the short shadow.

Ⓒ Both pictures show the flag at the end of the day.

11. Yoon sees different stars on a winter night than he sees on a summer night. Why?

Ⓐ You can see stars only in the winter sky.

Ⓑ Clouds may block the stars in summer.

Ⓒ You can see different stars in different seasons.

12. Which object can you see in both the daytime and nighttime skies?

Ⓐ

Ⓑ

Ⓒ

Inquiry and the Big Idea
Write the answers to these questions.

13. You want to get a closer look at the stars in the sky.

a. What tool can help you see the stars better?

_____

b. How does this tool help you?

_____

_____

14. Compare and contrast the stars and the moon.

a. What is one way they are the same?

_____

_____

b. Name a way they are different.

_____

_____

All About Matter

sandcastle

Big Idea

All objects are matter. Matter can change in different ways.

I Wonder Why

We use the words <u>brown</u> and <u>rough</u> to tell about this sandcastle. Why?
Turn the page to find out.

Here's Why Brown and rough are properties of the <u>sandcastle</u>. A property is one part of what something is like.

In this unit, you will explore this Big Idea, the Essential Questions, and the Investigations on the Inquiry Flipchart.

Levels of Inquiry Key ■ DIRECTED ■ GUIDED ■ INDEPENDENT

Track Your Progress

Big Idea All objects are matter. Matter can change in different ways.

Essential Questions

Now I Get the Big Idea!

Science Notebook

Before you begin each lesson, be sure to write your thoughts about the Essential Question.

Essential Question

What Can We Observe About Objects?

Engage Your Brain!

Find the answer to the question in the lesson.

How are the blocks in this rabbit the same?

They are all _Legos®_.

Active Reading

Lesson Vocabulary

1 Preview the lesson.

2 Write the 5 vocabulary terms here.

weight _matter_

proprtex _Texture_

teapretoher

325

Why Matter Matters

Look around. What do you see? Are there trees, toys, or books? These things are matter. **Matter** is anything that takes up space. Even the air you breathe is matter!

▶ Look at the ball, the clock, and the boy. Draw an X on each thing that is matter.

What's It Like?

A **property** of matter is one part of what something is like. Some properties are size, shape, color, and texture. **Texture** is what an object feels like.

Active Reading

Find the sentence that tells the meaning of property. Draw a line under the sentence.

Size

Big and **small** are words that tell about size.

Shape

Star and **heart** are words that tell about shape.

► **In each box, draw an X on the object that does not belong.**

Color

Red and **blue** are words that tell about color.

Texture

Soft and **hard** are words that tell about texture.

Heavy or Light?

Some things you pick up feel light.
Others feel heavy. **Weight** is the measure
of how heavy an object feels.

heavy

light

Do the Math!
Order by Weight

Order from light to heavy. Write 1 for lightest.
Write 3 for heaviest.

paint

paper clip

marker

_3_

_1_

Hot or Cold?

How hot is a pizza? How cold is an ice pop? You can find out by using temperature. **Temperature** is the measure of how warm something is.

pizza

ice pop

hot cocoa

lemonade

▶ Draw something hot.

▶ Draw something cold.

Will It Sink or Will It Float?

Think about things in a tub or a pool. A sponge may stay on top of the water. A bar of soap may go to the bottom.

An object that floats stays on top of a liquid. An object that sinks falls to the bottom.

►Circle what floats. Draw an X on what sinks.

The canoe with people is big and heavy.

Why does it float?

How Does That Boat Float?

Look at the clay boat and the clay ball. The ball sinks. The boat floats. Why? The ball and the boat have different shapes. The shape of the boat helps it float. Sometimes changing the shape of something makes it sink or float.

Sum It Up!

① Choose It!

Circle each blue shape. Draw an X on each square. Underline each big circle.

② Mark It!

Draw an X on the small dog.

③ Write It!

Is this toy soft or hard? Write the word.

_____

Name **DAViyai**

Word Play

Write the word from the box for each clue.

| property | weight | texture | temperature |

the measure of how warm something is

t e [m](1) p e r [a](2) t u r e

the way something feels

[t](3) e x [t](4) u r e

the measure of how heavy something feels

w [e](5) i g h t

a part of what something is like

p r o p e [r](6) t y

Solve the riddle. Write the circled letters in order on the lines below.

I am anything that takes up space.
What am I?   m a t t e r
     1   2   3   4   5   6

1 Sort these shapes. Draw each one in the diagram.

hearts   red

red hearts

2 Circle each thing that floats.

Draw an X on each thing that sinks.

3 Name or draw something hot. _____

Name or draw something cold. _____

Ask a Polymer Scientist

What are polymers?
Polymers are a kind of material. We can find some polymers, such as silk, in nature. Scientists make other polymers, such as plastics.

What does a polymer scientist do?
I work with different materials to make them better. Materials can cause problems. I try to solve the problems.

What is one problem that polymer scientists are working on?
Some polymers take years to break down. This makes a lot of garbage. Scientists want to make polymers that break down faster so there is less garbage.

Now It's Your Turn!

▶ **What question would you ask?**

_____

_____

_____

_____

Polymer Play

▶ **Think about what a polymer scientist studies. Make a list of polymers on the lines below.**

rubber ball

foam peanuts

plastic toy

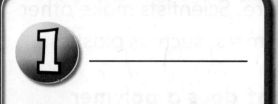
plastic bags

1 _____

2 _____

3 _____

4 _____

Fun Fact
A lobster's shell is a polymer.

Essential Question

What Are Solids, Liquids, and Gases?

Engage Your Brain!

Find the answer to the question in the lesson.

How is water different from stone and metal?

_____

Active Reading

Lesson Vocabulary
1 Preview the lesson.
2 Write the 5 vocabulary terms here.

_____   _____

_____   _____

_____

It All Matters

How are towels, water, and balloons the same? They are all matter.

Matter is anything that takes up space. It has mass. **Mass** is the amount of matter something has.

Matter may be different. Different kinds of matter are solids, liquids, and gases.

340

▶ Circle three things in this picture that are made of matter.

Do the Math!

Order by Mass

You can measure mass with a balance.

▶ Order the objects by mass. Write 1 for least mass. Write 3 for most mass.

book

marker

paint

_____   _____   _____

Solid as a Rock

A **solid** is a kind of matter that keeps its shape. The flip-flops and towels are solids. What happens if you move a flip-flop? It still keeps its shape.

What other solids could you find at a pool party?

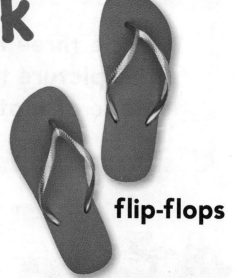

flip-flops

towels

Lovely Liquid

A **liquid** is matter that flows. It takes the shape of its container. Look at the juice. It pours from the pitcher to the glass. It takes the shape of each container.

juice

What a Gas!

A **gas** is the only kind of matter that fills all of the space in its container. It does not have its own shape. The gas in the balloons spreads to fill all the space.

balloons

bubbles

▶ **What kind of matter is inside the bubbles?**

_____

A Matter of Fact

▶ Write <u>yes</u> or <u>no</u> in the first four columns. In the last column, write <u>solid</u> or <u>liquid</u> to classify each one.

Are These Objects Solids or Liquids?

	Does it have mass?	Does it take up space?
lemonade	yes	yes
sunglasses	yes	yes
dish soap	yes	yes

Does it have its own shape?	Does it take the shape of its container?	Is it a solid or a liquid?
no	Yes	liquid
Yes	no	solid
no	yes	liqid

Sum It Up!

① Circle It!

Circle the objects that are solids.

② Draw It!

Draw something that is a liquid.

③ Write It!

Write the answer to the riddle.

I am a kind of matter you might know.

I spread out and seem to grow.

I have mass and take up space.

Put me in a case and I fill the case.

What am I? _____

346

Name _____

Word Play

Color each solid red. Color each liquid blue. Color each gas yellow.

Apply Concepts

Write to complete the chart.

Solids, Liquids, and Gases

Kind of Matter	Definition
solid	• _____ _____
_____	• flows • takes the shape of its container
_____	• fills all the space in its container

Write to complete the sentence.

All matter has _____

and takes up _____.

Take It Home!

Family Members: Have your child classify objects as solids, liquids, or gases. Ask your child to explain the clues he or she used to classify each object.

Name _____

Essential Question

How Can We Measure Temperature?

Set a Purpose
Tell what you will find out.

_____

Think About the Procedure

1 How will you test whether light colors or dark colors warm up faster?

_____

_____

2 How do you know which color warms up faster?

_____

_____

Record Your Data

In this chart, record the temperature at the beginning and the temperature after 30 minutes.

Color	Beginning Temperature	Temperature After 30 Minutes
White		
Black		

Draw Conclusions

Do light colors or dark colors warm up faster?

_____

Ask More Questions

What other questions about temperature could you test and measure?

_____

_____

_____

350

Essential Question

How Can Matter Change?

Engage Your Brain!

Find the answer to the question in the lesson.

How were the foods changed to make the giraffe?

_____

Active Reading

Lesson Vocabulary

1 Preview the lesson.

2 Write the 2 vocabulary terms here.

_____   _____

Make a Change

All matter has properties. A property is one part of what something is like. Cutting and folding can change the properties of matter. Breaking and tearing can change the properties of matter, too.

Active Reading

A cause tells why something happens. Circle words that name actions that cause changes to properties of matter.

cutting

© Houghton Mifflin Harcourt Publishing Company   (b) ©moodboard/Corbis

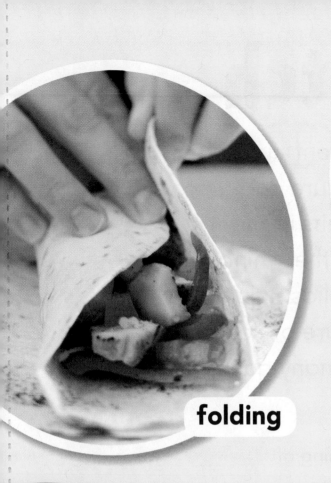

folding

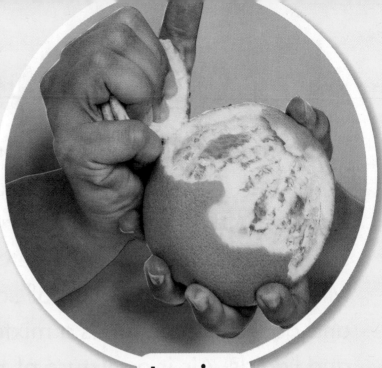

tearing

breaking

▶ Think of a food.
Draw a way you can
change it.

Mix and Match

A **mixture** is a mix of different kinds of matter. The parts of the mixture do not become new things. The fruits in the salad mix but do not become other things. Mixtures may be made up of solids, liquids, and gases. Lemonade is a mixture of solids and liquids. Air is a mixture of many gases.

Active Reading

Find the sentence that tells the meaning of **mixture**. Draw a line under that sentence.

strawberry

orange

grape

pineapple

▶ Label each part of the fruit salad. Then tell why it is a mixture.

_____

_____

Stir and See

Matter changes when it dissolves. To **dissolve** is to completely mix a solid with a liquid. Sugar and salt dissolve in water.

Adding or taking away heat may change how matter dissolves. Some matter dissolves more quickly in warm or hot water.

Many liquids mix when put together. Others, such as oil and water, separate when mixed.

▶Circle <u>dissolves</u> or <u>separates</u> to tell what happens.

dissolves   separates

dissolves   separates

357

Sum It Up!

① Write It!

Write two ways you can change matter.

_____

_____

_____

② Circle It!

Circle the word that best describes the picture.

mixture   dissolve

③ Mark It!

Mark an X on each thing that dissolves in water.

Name _____

Word Play

Write the word that tells about each set of pictures.

dissolves	mixture	separates

 +  =

_____

 +  =

_____

 +  =

_____

Apply Concepts

Write a word to match each set of clues.

| makes a solid mix completely with a liquid | → |
| may happen more quickly in warm or hot water | → |

_____

| may be made up of solids, liquids, or gases | → |
| parts do not become new things | → |

_____

Name _____

Essential Question

What Dissolves in Water?

Set a Purpose
Tell what you want to find out.

_____

_____

Think About the Procedure
1 How do you know when a substance dissolves in water?

_____

2 Why do you predict and repeat the activity with cold water?

_____

_____

Record Your Data

Record your observations in the chart.

What I Stirred	Warm Water	Cold Water
salt		
sugar		

Draw Conclusions

Did salt and sugar dissolve in warm water?

_____

What was the difference between dissolving in warm water and dissolving in cold water?

_____

Ask More Questions

What other questions could you ask about dissolving?

_____

_____

_____

High Tech!

Classroom Technology

Engineers make technology to meet needs and solve problems. Some things you could not do without technology.

Look at the picture. What do these things help you do at school?

clock

computer

scissors

pencils

pencil sharpener

stapler

High-Tech Home

You use technology at home, too. Draw one thing you use. Write about what it helps you do.

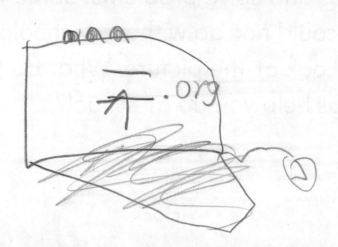

to lean.

Build On It!

Make an object better. Complete **Redesign It: Better Technology** on the Inquiry Flipchart.

Unit 9 Review

Vocabulary Review

Use the terms in the box to complete the sentences.

| dissolve |
| property |
| solid |

1. One part of what something is like is a _____.

2. Mixing salt with water causes the salt to _____.

3. A kind of matter that keeps its shape is a _____.

Science Concepts

Fill in the letter of the choice that best answers the question.

4. How is all matter the **same**?

   Ⓐ All matter is solid.

   Ⓑ All matter takes up space.

   Ⓒ All matter is made from natural materials.

5. You put soft toys in one pile. You put hard toys in another pile. How did you sort?

   Ⓐ by color

   Ⓑ by size

   Ⓒ by texture

6. Which cup has the hottest water?

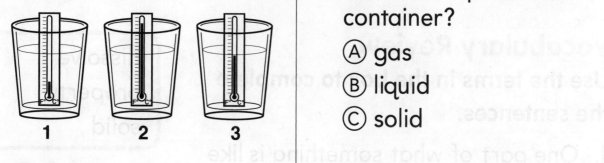

1   2   3

Ⓐ Cup 1
Ⓑ Cup 2
Ⓒ Cup 3

7. Which kind of matter fills all the space of its container?
Ⓐ gas
Ⓑ liquid
Ⓒ solid

8. You see several objects at a party. Which object is a liquid?
Ⓐ apple juice
Ⓑ a cake
Ⓒ the air in a balloon

9. Which does sugar dissolve more easily in?

Ⓐ in cold water

Ⓑ in cool water

Ⓒ in warm water

10. How do you know that the material being poured is a liquid and not a solid?

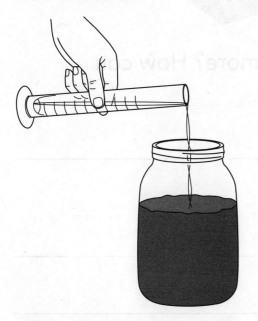

Ⓐ It has mass.

Ⓑ It has its own shape.

Ⓒ It flows and takes the shape of its container.

11. How is the person changing the blanket?

Ⓐ The person is melting the blanket.

Ⓑ The person is folding the blanket.

Ⓒ The person is cutting the blanket.

12. Which is a mixture?

Ⓐ grapes

Ⓑ pencils

Ⓒ salad

Inquiry and the Big Idea
Write the answers to these questions.

13. These two containers started with water at 25 °C.

    They both stayed in the sun for 30 minutes.

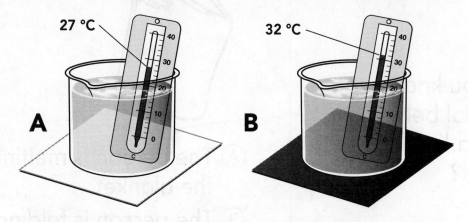

27 °C   A   32 °C   B

a. Which container heated up more? How can you tell?

_____

b. Why did this happen?

_____

_____

14. Does salt dissolve in water? How do you know?

_____

_____

_____

Forces and Energy

Big Idea

Forces change the way objects move. Sound is energy that you hear.

Indianapolis Colts kicker

I Wonder Why

The ball changes position when the kicker kicks it. Why? *Turn the page to find out.*

Here's Why The ball changes position because of the force from the kicker's foot.

In this unit, you will explore this Big Idea, the Essential Questions, and the Investigations on the Inquiry Flipchart.

Levels of Inquiry Key ■ DIRECTED ■ GUIDED ■ INDEPENDENT

Track Your Progress

Big Idea Forces change the way objects move. Sound is energy that you hear.

Essential Questions

Now I Get the Big Idea!

Science Notebook

Before you begin each lesson, be sure to write your thoughts about the Essential Question.

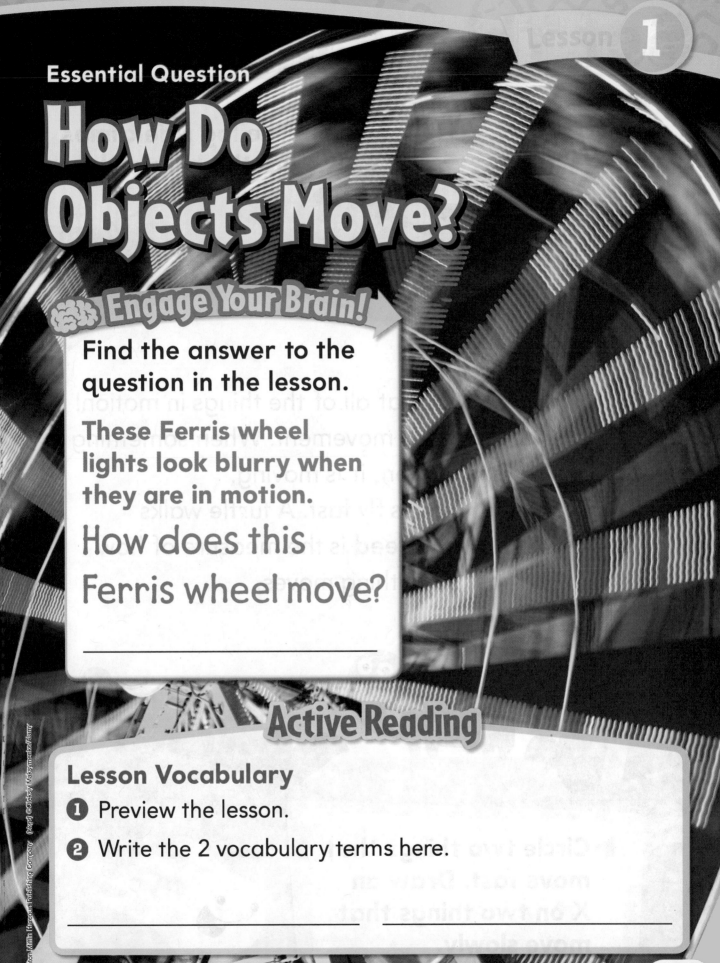

Essential Question

How Do Objects Move?

Engage Your Brain!

Find the answer to the question in the lesson.

These Ferris wheel lights look blurry when they are in motion.

How does this Ferris wheel move?

_____

Active Reading

Lesson Vocabulary

① Preview the lesson.

② Write the 2 vocabulary terms here.

_____ _____

Set Things in Motion

The log ride climbs up the hill slowly.

log ride

Look at all of the things in motion! **Motion** is movement. When something is in motion, it is moving.

Planes fly fast. A turtle walks slowly. **Speed** is the measure of how fast something moves.

▶ Circle two things that move fast. Draw an X on two things that move slowly.

Do the Math!
Make a Bar Graph

Pam went on three rides. This graph shows how long she waited for each ride.

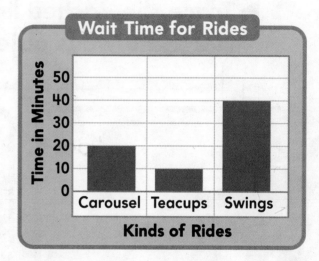

Wait Time for Rides

Time in Minutes

50
40
30
20
10
0

Carousel Teacups Swings

Kinds of Rides

Use the graph to answer the questions.

1. Which ride had the shortest wait?

   teacups

2. How does the graph tell you?

   bars

The log ride zooms down the hill fast.

It's Your Move!

Objects can move in many ways.
They can move in a straight line, zigzag,
back and forth, or round and round.

▶ **Trace the dashed lines below to
show the ways objects can move.**

straight line

zigzag

Active Reading

A detail is a fact about a main idea. Draw one line under a detail. Draw an arrow to the main idea it tells about.

back and forth

round and round

Sum It Up!

① Draw It!

Read the label in each box.
Draw an arrow to show the kind of motion.

back and forth

zigzag

round and round

straight line

② Circle It!

Look at each pair of objects.
Circle the one that goes fast.

Name _____

Word Play

Work your way through the maze to match the word with its meaning.

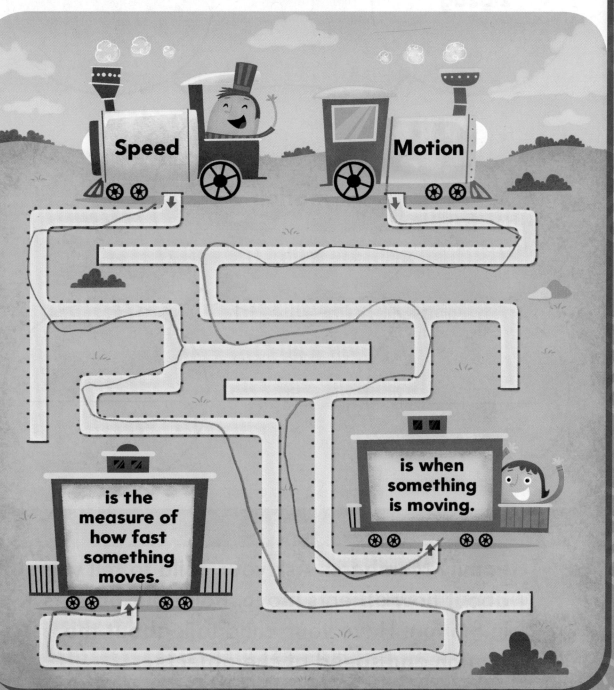

Speed

Motion

is the measure of how fast something moves.

is when something is moving.

Apply Concepts

Complete the word web below.

The Way Things Move

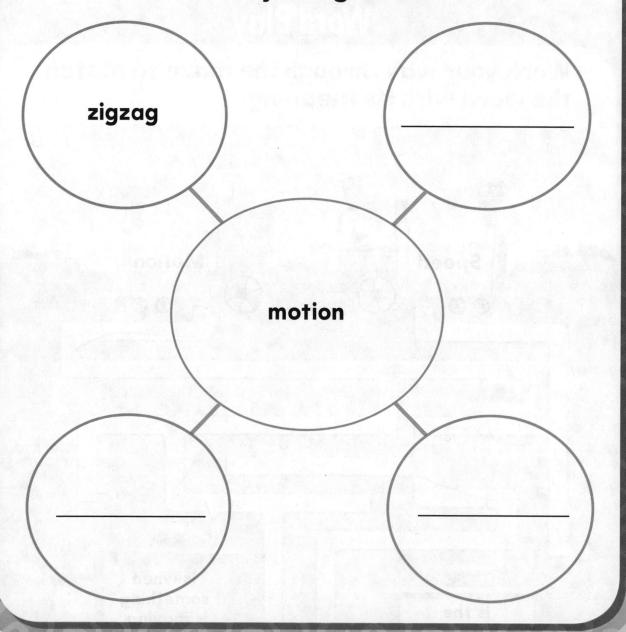

zigzag

_____

motion

_____

_____

Take It Home!

Family Members: Ask your child to tell you about how objects move. Point out objects in motion. Have your child talk about the motion and speed of the objects.

Essential Question

How Can We Change the Way Objects Move?

Engage Your Brain!

Find the answer to the question in the lesson.

How is pushing a swing like pulling a wagon?

A push and a pull are both

_____.

Active Reading

Lesson Vocabulary

1 Preview the lesson.

2 Write the 3 vocabulary terms here.

_____ _____

_____

In Full Force

What makes the wagon move? The girl gives it a push. A **push** moves an object away from you. The boy gives the wagon a pull. A **pull** moves an object closer to you.

Pushes and pulls are forces. A **force** makes an object move or stop moving. When the girl and boy push and pull the wagon, it starts to move.

► **Draw yourself pushing something.**

► Draw yourself
pulling something.

Active Reading

Find the sentence that tells the meaning
of **force**. Draw a line under the sentence.

Using Force

Look at the pictures. How does a force move a ball? A force can change the way an object moves. It can change a ball's speed or direction.

Changing Speed

Force can change an object's speed. It can make something start moving or stop moving. It can make something go faster or more slowly.

▶ **What is going to happen to the ball?**

_____

_____

You can kick a ball to make it start moving or go faster.

You can catch a ball to stop it.

▶ Describe how the motion of the car changes.

1

2

3

1 _____

2 _____

3 _____

What Is Your Position?

Look at the pictures. Things are moving up and down. They are moving in and out. Position words tell where something is. Some position words are **in, out, up, down, left,** and **right**.

A force can move something to a new position.

Active Reading

A detail is a fact about a main idea. Draw one line under a detail. Draw an arrow to the main idea it tells about.

up

down

in

out

A Step in the Right Direction

Think about pushing a friend on a swing. Your friend moves away from you and then comes back. Forces can move things toward you and away from you. A force can change the direction of an object.

▶ **Tell how the direction of this swing changes.**

_____

_____

_____

What Makes That Coaster Move?

Roller coasters are fun! They go up and down, fast and slow, round and round. People on the ride might yell as they change speed and direction. What makes the coaster move?

A motor pulls a chain. The chain pulls the car up the first hill.

Gravity is the force that pulls the car down. Gravity pulls all things toward Earth.

▶ **What pulls the car down the hill?**

_____

Sum It Up!

① Solve It!

Write the word that solves the riddle.

I move a box
when it is full.
I can be
a push or a pull.

What am I?

_____

② Circle It!

Forces can change objects. Circle the words that tell the kinds of changes.

speed   color

size   direction

shape

③ Label It!

Write __push__ or __pull__ to label each picture.

_____   _____

388

Name _____

Word Play

Complete the letter by using these words.

speed	push	force	pull

Dear Jen,

We moved into our new house. My dad drove the moving truck. He made sure the _____ of the truck was not too fast.

Moving is hard! I had to _____ boxes all day. It took a huge _____ to move my box of toys. My dad had to _____ it while my brother pushed.

Your friend,

Amy

Apply Concepts

Complete the chart. Write a word on each blank line.

Cause		Effect
Force	▶	moves a _____.
Force	▶	makes a wagon go _____.
Force	▶	pushes a swing _____ from you.
Force	▶	moves a book to a new _____ on a shelf.

Take It Home!

Family Members: Ask your child to tell you about forces and motion. Have your child point out examples of pushes and pulls and explain how those forces change motion.

1 He is known for observing an apple falling from a tree.

4 Things to Know About Isaac Newton

2 He wrote his Three Laws of Motion.

3 His laws help us understand why things move the way they do.

4 He was one of the greatest scientists in history.

Objects in Motion

▶ Think about what you know about Isaac Newton. Then write the answer to each question.

What did Isaac Newton write after seeing an apple fall from a tree?

_____

_____

What is Isaac Newton remembered as?

_____

_____

What do the Three Laws of Motion tell us?

_____

_____

Name _____

Essential Question

How Can We Change Motion?

Set a Purpose
Tell what you want to figure out in this activity.

_____

_____

Think About the Procedure
❶ What do you want to do to the cube?

_____

❷ List some ideas for how to push the cube.

_____

❸ List some ideas for how to pull the cube.

_____

Record Your Data

Write or draw to show what you did.

Action	What I Did
Push	
Pull	

Draw Conclusions

How do the string, straw, and stick change the motion of the cube?

_____

_____

Ask More Questions

What are some other questions you could ask about changing the motion of a cube?

_____

_____

Essential Question

What Is Sound?

Engage Your Brain!

Find the answer to the question in the lesson.

What kind of sound does this police car make?

a _____ sound

Active Reading

Lesson Vocabulary

❶ Preview the lesson.

❷ Write the 4 vocabulary terms here.

_____   _____

_____   _____

Sounds All Around

Listen. What do you hear? Is it a person talking? Is it a pencil tapping? Both are sounds. **Sound** is a kind of energy you hear.

Active Reading

Find the sentence that tells the meaning of **sound**. Draw a line under the sentence.

Sound is made when an object vibrates. To **vibrate** is to move quickly back and forth.

The strings on a guitar vibrate when you pluck them.

The top of a drum vibrates when you hit it.

▶ **Touch your throat and hum. What happens?**

_____

Loud or Soft

Some sounds are loud. Other sounds are soft. **Loudness** is how loud or soft a sound is. A loud sound can make you cover your ears. A soft sound can be hard to hear.

Active Reading

When things are contrasted, you find out ways they are different. Draw triangles around two things that are being contrasted.

An instrument can make a loud or a soft sound. Its loudness changes with how you play it. A drum makes a louder sound if you hit it harder.

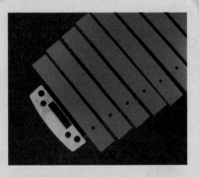

high pitch

low pitch

**Some sounds are high.
Some sounds are low.
Pitch is how high or
low a sound is.**

▶ **Look at the xylophone.**

1. Which bars have a low pitch?

the _____ bars

2. Which bars have a high pitch?

the _____ bars

Listen Up!

Sound is important to everyday life. Some sounds give you information. People talk to each other to learn things. A dog's bark may let you know that a person is coming. Sounds can warn you, too. A smoke detector warns of a fire.

What do these sounds tell you?

▶ **Draw an X on the picture that tells you someone is at the door.**

Sum It Up!

① Mark It!

Circle the place where people are quiet.
Draw an X on the place where people are loud.

② Choose It!

Circle the bell with a higher pitch.

③ Draw It!

Draw an object that makes a warning sound.

402

Name _____

Word Play

Unscramble the word to complete each sentence.

| pitch | sound | vibrate | loudness |

1. dnsuo   A ___ ___ ___ ___ ___ is a kind of energy that you hear.

2. bivtare   To ___ ___ ___ ___ ___ ___ ___ is to move quickly back and forth.

3. doulsens   A sound's ___ ___ ___ ___ ___ ___ ___ ___ is how loud or soft it is.

4. ctpih   A sound's ___ ___ ___ ___ ___ is how high or low it is.

Apply Concepts

Write to complete the chart.

1.

Kind of Sound	Example
loud	hammer banging
soft	
high	bird chirping
low	

Answer the question below.

2. What warning sounds have you heard? Write a sentence about one of them.

_____

_____

_____

Take It Home!

Family Members: Take a walk outside with your child. Ask your child to describe the loudness and pitch of the sounds you hear.

Name _____

Essential Question

How Do We Make Sound?

Set a Purpose

Tell what you want to do.

_____

_____

Think About the Procedure

1 How will you use your telephone?

_____

_____

2 What will you do with the string as you talk?

_____

_____

Record Your Data

Write in the chart to tell what you heard.

How We Held the String	What We Heard
tight	
loose	

Draw Conclusions

What did you infer would happen when you held the string loose? Why do you think the sound changed?

_____

_____

_____

Ask More Questions

What other questions could you ask about the string telephone?

_____

_____

Fly to the Sky

The First Flight

Wilbur and Orville Wright were brothers and inventors. They flew the first airplane. First, they made designs of their plane. Next, they built it. Then, they tested it. After a few tries, their plane flew. The flight lasted only 12 seconds.

This is one of the Wright Brothers' planes.

Today's planes can fly much longer and have more parts.

Plane Parts

Each part of a plane has a job to do. The
wings help lift it. The tail keeps it flying straight.
The propeller moves the plane forward.

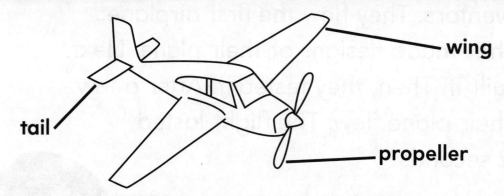

tail

wing

propeller

Use the picture of the plane to answer the questions.

① Which part keeps the plane flying straight? Circle it.

② What would happen if the wings on the plane were
missing? Explain.

_____

_____

Build On It!

Build your own paper airplanes. Complete
Build It: Paper Airplanes on the Inquiry Flipchart.

Unit 10 Review

Name _____

Vocabulary Review
Use the terms in the box to complete the sentences.

> motion
> pitch
> push

1. A force that moves an object away from you is a

   _____.

2. Whether a sound is high or low is the sound's _____.

3. If something is moving, it is in

   _____.

Science Concepts
Fill in the letter of the choice that best answers the question.

4. Which of these forces is a push?
   - (A) lifting a bag
   - (B) opening a drawer
   - (C) hitting a ball

5. What is speed?
   - (A) the measure of how fast something moves
   - (B) the measure of ways something moves
   - (C) the measure of where something is

6. Which moves the fastest?

(A)

(B)

(C)

7. You need something that can hit a ball over a net. What should you ask?

(A) What material is the ball made of?

(B) What object will put a force on the ball?

(C) What colors are the object and the ball?

8. A player catches a ball in her hand. What puts a force on the ball?

(A) the ball itself

(B) the player's hand

(C) the player's eyes

9. A ball is hanging from a string. You pull the ball back and let it go. What kind of motion does the ball make?

Ⓐ back and forth

Ⓑ round and round

Ⓒ straight line

10. What can a force do?

Ⓐ stop an object

Ⓑ move an object

Ⓒ move or stop an object

11. How is sound made on this instrument?

Ⓐ The handle vibrates.

Ⓑ The strings vibrate.

Ⓒ The wood vibrates.

12. Which words describe how a force can change an object's position?

Ⓐ fast or slow

Ⓑ right or left

Ⓒ short or long

Inquiry and the Big Idea

Write the answers to these questions.

13. How does a bell make sound when it is rung?

_____

14. Look at the picture.

a. What type of force is being put on the ball? How do you know?

_____

_____

b. Name two things that the force can change about the ball.

_____

Interactive Glossary

This Interactive Glossary will help you learn how to spell a vocabulary term. The Glossary will give you the meaning of the term. It will also show you a picture to help you understand what the term means.

Where you see **Your Turn** write your own words or draw your own picture to help you remember what the term means.

A

amphibian

The group of animals that begin life in water. Most grown amphibians live on land. (p. 113)

Your Turn

B

bird

The group of animals with feathers on their bodies and wings. Most birds can fly. (p. 111)

C

cone

The part of a nonflowering plant that holds the plant's seeds. (p. 161)

Interactive Glossary

D

design process
A plan with steps that helps engineers find good solutions. (p. 49)

dissolve
To completely mix a solid with a liquid. (p. 356)

E

engineer
Someone who uses math and science to solve problems. (p. 48)

environment
All the living and nonliving things in a place. (pp. 88, 176)

Your Turn

F

fish

The group of animals that lives in water and gets oxygen through gills. Fish have scales and use fins to swim. (p. 114)

flower

The part of a plant that makes seeds. (pp. 147, 160)

food chain

A path that shows how energy moves from plants to animals. (p. 182)

Your Turn

Interactive Glossary

force

Something that makes an object move or stop moving. (p. 380)

fruit

The part of the plant that holds seeds. (p. 147)

G

gas

A kind of matter that fills all the space of its container. (p. 343)

Your Turn

I

gills

The parts of a fish that take in oxygen from the water. (p. 95)

gills →

inquiry skills

Skills that help you find out information. (p. 18)

Falling Leaves Forest

observe

compare

H

human-made

Materials made by people. (p. 66)

insect

A kind of animal that has three body parts and six legs. (p. 115)

Your Turn

Interactive Glossary

investigation
A test that scientists do. (p. 30)

leaf
The part of a plant that makes food for the plant. A leaf uses light, air, and water to make food. (p. 146)

Your Turn

L

lake
A body of fresh water with land all around it. (p. 227)

liquid
A kind of matter that flows and takes the shape of its container. (p. 342)

M

living things

Things that are living. People, animals, and plants are living things because they need food, water, air, and space to live. They grow, change, and reproduce. (p. 84)

magnify

To make something look bigger. (p. 298)

Your Turn

loudness

How loud or soft a sound is. (p. 398)

Interactive Glossary

mammal
The group of animals with fur or hair on their bodies. (p. 110)

Your Turn

mass
The amount of matter in an object. (p. 340)

materials
What objects are made of. (p. 64)

matter

Anything that takes up space. (pp. 326, 340)

mixture

A mix of different kinds of matter. (p. 354)

moon

A large sphere, or ball, of rock. (p. 296)

Interactive Glossary

motion

Movement. When something is in motion, it is moving. (p. 372)

natural resource

Anything from nature that people can use. (p. 200)

Your Turn

N

natural

Materials found in nature. (p. 66)

nonliving things

Things that are not alive. Nonliving things do not need food, air, and water. They do not grow and change. (p. 86)

O

ocean

A large body of salty water. (p. 228)

Your Turn

nutrients

Things in soil that help plants grow. (p. 134)

P

phases

The shapes of the moon you see as it moves. (p. 309)

Interactive Glossary

pitch
How high or low a sound is. (p. 399)

property
One part of what something is like. Color, size, and shape are each a property. (pp. 212, 328)

Your Turn

pollution
Waste that harms land, water, and air. (p. 238)

pull
To move an object closer to you. (p. 380)

push

To move an object away from you. (p. 380)

reduce

To use less of a resource. (p. 242)

R

recycle

To use the materials in old things to make new things. (p. 242)

reproduce

To make new living things like oneself. (p. 84)

Interactive Glossary

reptile

The group of animals with dry skin covered in scales. (p. 112)

Your Turn

river

A large body of flowing water. (p. 226)

rock

A hard, nonliving object from the ground. (p. 204)

reuse

To use a resource again. (p. 242)

roots

The part of a plant that holds the plant in place. The roots take in water and nutrients. (p. 144)

S

science tools

Tools people use to find out about things. (p. 8)

seed

The part of a plant that new plants grow from. (p. 147)

season

A time of year that has a certain kind of weather. The four seasons are spring, summer, fall, and winter. (p. 274)

Your Turn

senses

The way you observe and learn. The five senses are sight, hearing, smell, taste, and touch. (p. 4)

Interactive Glossary

shadow
A dark place made where an object blocks light. (p. 307)

soil
The top layer of Earth. It is made up of small pieces of rock and once-living things. (pp. 134, 205)

shelter
A place where an animal can be safe. (pp. 96, 176)

solid
The only kind of matter that keeps its shape. (p. 342)

Your Turn

sound

Energy you can hear. (p. 396)

star

An object in the sky that gives off its own light. The sun is the closest star to Earth. (p. 294)

Your Turn

speed

The measure of how fast something moves. (p. 372)

stem

The part of a plant that holds up the plant. (p. 145)

Interactive Glossary

stream
A small body of flowing water. (p. 226)

sun
The star closest to Earth. (p. 294)

sunlight
Light that comes from the sun. (p. 132)

T

telescope
A tool that helps magnify things in the sky. (p. 298)

temperature

A measure of how hot or cold something is. (pp. 260, 331)

Your Turn

texture

What an object feels like. (pp. 216, 328)

V

vibrate

To move quickly back and forth. (p. 397)

W

weather

What the air outside is like. (p. 258)

Interactive Glossary

weather pattern

A change in the weather that repeats. (p. 274)

weight

The measure of how heavy an object feels. (p. 330)

wind

Air that moves. (p. 258)

Index

Index

Index

Index

windshield wipers,
39–40

winter season, 255,
280–281

Wright, Wilbur and
Orville, 407

zoo keeper, 123–124